Nina Osswald, Christoph Dittrich

**Sustainable Food Consumption and Urban Lifestyles**

The case of Hyderabad/India

*Emerging megacities*
*Dicussion Papers*
Edited by Konrad Hagedorn, Christine Werthmann, Dimitrios Zikos, Ramesh Chennamaneni

Humboldt-Universität zu Berlin
Department of Agricultural Economics
Division of Resource Economics
Philippstr. 13, House 12
10115 Berlin

Tel.: +49 (0)30 2093 6305
Fax: +49 (0)30 2093 6497
www.agrar.hu-berlin.de/struktur/institute/wisola/fg/ress
www.sustainable-hyderabad.de

Contact: emerging.megacities@hu-berlin.de

The emerging megacities discussion papers are available at:
www.eh-verlag.de

ISSN print edition 2193-6927

*Emerging megacities Discussion Papers* are prepared by researchers working on topics in the realm of sustainable development in Megacities of Tomorrow, a research priority by the German Ministry of Education and Research (BMBF). The papers have been peer-reviewed by a board of external reviewers.
Views and opinions expressed do not necessarily represent those of the Division of Resource Economics.
Comments are highly welcome and should be sent directly to the authors.
We welcome contributions on any topics related to Megacities of Tomorrow. Further information on the submission procedure is given at:
*www.sustainable-hyderabad.de/emerging-megacities*

Osswald, Nina; Dittrich, Christoph

Sustainable Food Consumption and Urban Lifestyles
*The case of Hyderabad/India*

Emerging megacities Discussion Papers, Volume 3/2010

ISBN/EAN: 978-3-86741-820-1

First published in 2012 by Europaeischer Hochschulverlag GmbH & Co KG, Bremen, Germany.

© Europaeischer Hochschulverlag GmbH & Co KG, Fahrenheitstr. 1, D-28359 Bremen (www.eh-verlag.de). All rights reserved.

Cover: Photo "Metropolis", ferendus (flickr). Creative Commons License

No part of this publication may be reproduced or transmitted, in any form or by any means, electronic, mechanical, photocopying, recording or otherwise, or stored in any retrieval system of nay nature, without the written permission of the copyright holder and the publisher, application for which shall be made to the publisher.

EHV

# Sustainable Food Consumption and Urban Lifestyles
## The case of Hyderabad/ India

*Nina Osswald*[*], *Christoph Dittrich*[*†]

July 2010

## Abstract

The lifestyles and food consumption patterns of India's new urban middle classes are changing rapidly. Emerging trends such as the growing popularity of fast food and convenience food and the increasing consumption of animal products, sugar and fat are causing adverse environmental, health and social effects. In order to counter these trends, effective strategies for promoting sustainable food consumption patterns are urgently needed.

This empirical case study combines a revised update of the study "The Market for Organic Food: Consumer Attitudes and Marketing Opportunities" (Osswald and Dittrich 2009) with a broader perspective on the socio-cultural contexts of sustainable food consumption. The study outlines how "sustainable food choices" can be defined in the Indian context, and examines spatial structures of the market for products from sustainable agriculture in the South Indian emerging megacity of Hyderabad. It explores socio-cultural contexts of sustainable food consumption, outlines target groups for marketing organic food and identifies obstacles to sustainable food consumption.

The findings point to a moderate but growing demand for organic food, especially among the middle classes. Availability is limited and not able to satisfy the demand at this stage. Most consumers are motivated almost exclusively by health considerations; awareness of the links between environmental problems and food choices is low. Based on these findings, the report assesses the potential for future development of the organic segment as part of a sustainable urban food system, and develops recommendations for action in order to promote sustainable food consumption in Hyderabad.

***Key words:*** *organic food, urban middle class, sustainable food consumption, Hyderabad, India*

---

[*] Institute of Geography, Dept. of Human Geography, University of Goettingen, Goldschmidtstrasse 5, 37077 Goettingen
[†] Corresponding author. Tel.: +49 551 398 021. Email: christoph.dittrich@geo.uni-goettingen.de

# 1 Introduction

## 1.1 Challenges to a Sustainable Urban Food System

In India, 28 % of the population live in cities (Census 2001), and this number is growing continuously due to migration and population growth, especially in economically highly dynamic cities like Mumbai, Bangalore and Hyderabad. These rapidly growing megacities face manifold challenges, from climate change and environmental pollution to urban infrastructure development, public health and food security. Many of these challenges are intricately linked with urban food systems. A food system can be defined as the spatial, functional, social and environmental integration of four sub-systems: production, distribution/ exchange, marketing/ delivery, and consumption of food. It comprises all biophysical and socioeconomic processes and relationships involved in these subsystems (Cannon 2002; CIAS 1995).

Over the past decades, the food system of the South Indian emerging megacity Hyderabad has been undergoing a number of changes connected with trends of industrialisation, economic liberalisation and globalisation. These developments cause challenges to the food system's sustainability, which can be traced through several stages along the value chain of food products, from production to end consumption. Firstly, at the production stage of the food system the expansion of intensive conventional agriculture has depleted the natural resource base of many parts of rural India. While the Green Revolution technology succeeded in tremendously increasing production levels for a certain period of time, it also "led to the poverty of the soil and the people" due to its reductionist approach (DDS 2008: 3). Soils have been degraded and polluted with chemical pesticides and synthetic fertilisers, and biodiversity has been diminished. The high consumption of fossil fuels for producing synthetic pesticides and fertilisers contributes significantly to global warming. For producers, conventional farming poses severe health risks due to exposure to toxic chemicals in the field. Every year, Warangal District in Eastern Andhra Pradesh records over one thousand cases of pesticide poisoning and hundreds of deaths (Rao et al. 2005). Chemical residues in food products are endangering food safety, and the nutritional quality of conventionally grown food products decreases due to soil degradation.

Secondly, at the distribution and marketing stage, the globalisation of the economy and changes in urban purchasing patterns have led to longer supply chains and a marked increase in the number of supermarkets. Longer supply chains have caused a rise in energy used for transportation and temporary storage. In urban India, current trends in food retailing are largely the result of the preference of young and affluent consumers for shopping in malls and supermarkets. These retailing formats with their sophisticated infrastructure such as lighting and cooling facilities use more energy than traditional formats such as markets, Kirana stores or street vendors.

Thirdly, at the consumption stage of the food value chain, dietary changes among urban consumers have also led to increased energy consumption. While undernourishment is still a major problem among lower-income groups, there is a greater variety of food available to the higher-income groups than ever before, and eating out is increasingly fashionable as consumerism has become a new status symbol. An emerging trend towards eating more meat has adverse health effects and increases the ecological footprint of food consumption. The growing popularity of processed and convenience food[1] and fast food that are rich in sugar and fat have led to an increase in nutrition-related health problems such as secondary malnutrition, obesity and diabetes. As a reaction or countermovement, a new health consciousness has started to emerge among some consumers. However, there is a general lack of knowledge about what kind of food is healthy:

> *While food security does exist for Indian middle-classes due to their high standard of living, food safety does not, due to the lack of knowledge and a lack of availability of healthy food. An improvement towards food security as well as food safety for all strata of urban India is one of the biggest challenges Hyderabad has to face over the next few years* (Lohr and Dittrich 2007: 28).

In order to meet these various challenges, there is an urgent need to develop holistic and effective strategies for promoting sustainable consumption. All of the above trends are already causing high costs for society, for example in the form of externalised environmental costs of conventional farming, health problems and losses through inefficient supply chains. Each of the subsystems of a food system from production, distribution and marketing to consumption can thus make specific contributions to its environmental, economic and social sustainability.

Sustainable agriculture and successful marketing of the products derived from such farming systems can be one central element of a sustainable urban food system, especially when they are embedded in a decentralised, low-emission local food network. Sustainable agriculture improves environmental conditions in rural areas and contributes to climate

---

[1] Third-level processed or convenience foods are products that are ready to consume (ready-to-heat, ready-to-eat or ready-to-drink).

change mitigation and adaptation. It also reduces farmers' dependencies on external inputs and agrochemical corporations, improves food security and strengthens rural communities. For urban consumers, organic food can help meeting the challenge of achieving food security, food safety and healthy diets.

The total area currently under organic cultivation worldwide is more than 24 million hectares, and global demand for organic food is growing, with high growth rates estimated at somewhere between 10–15 % (Garibay and Jyoti 2003). At this stage, demand is concentrated primarily in regions like the USA, Europe and Japan. Developing countries and countries in transition are mainly exporters of organic food. The Indian domestic market for organic food is still in an early stage of its development, and commercial production in India is mostly targeted towards exports. However, the importance of organic farming and domestic demand are both growing rapidly. The successful realisation of the First BioFach India organic trade fair in Mumbai in November 2009 was an internationally visible indication of this development. Availability and commercial demand for organic products are concentrated mainly in the metropolitan centres, with Hyderabad lagging somewhat behind other megacities like Delhi, Mumbai or Bangalore (Rao et al. 2006).

In light of increasing numbers of affluent, quality-conscious consumers in the newly emerging urban middle classes and the recent trend towards health food, the domestic market in India has a huge potential and has been called a "sleeping giant" (Eyhorn 2005: 74). A survey conducted by the International Competence Centre for Organic Agriculture (ICCOA) in 2006 in the top eight metropolitan areas of the country (Rao et al. 2006) estimated the accessible market potential for organic foods at INR 5,620 million (USD122 million), and the overall market potential at about INR 14,520 million. In the medium to long term, the organic segment is expected to grow to 5–6 % of the overall food and grocery market (Menon, Sema, and Partap 2010: 75). In which way this potential will be developed in the future, and whether organic market growth will also lead to more sustainability, will depend largely on developments in the urban consumer market: supply and marketing strategies on the one hand, and consumer behaviour on the other.

## 1.2 Objectives and Structure of the Study

Since the study "The Market for Organic Food in Hyderabad/ India: Consumer Attitudes and Marketing Opportunities" (Osswald and Dittrich 2009) was completed in May 2009, several developments in the organic food sector of Hyderabad have made an update necessary. For example, many supermarkets have taken up organic food in their product range, and the local organic movement has received a new impulse through the inauguration and opening of a shop of the Sahaja Aharam Organic Consumer Cooperative. In addition, insights on market structures and marketing opportunities could be deepened through additional expert interviews conducted in 2010.

More than just providing an update, this study also expands both the empirical scope and the thematic focus of the previous study. Thematically, the focus was broadened from organic food to sustainable food consumption in more general terms. Since the establishment of the Indian National Standards for Organic Products (NSOP), only officially certified products can be sold as "organic". However, certification is not very well established yet, especially among resource-poor small farmers that form the bulk of the agricultural producers, nor is it well-known among consumers. In many regions, various other forms of sustainable agriculture, for example Non-Pesticide Management, play a more important role than certified organic production. An increase in the consumption of sustainable agriculture products is a vital component of a sustainable urban food system and can contribute to meeting many of the challenges outlined above. However, organic farming does not guarantee that the entire value chain of a food product or people's habits of food consumption are sustainable in a holistic sense. Therefore other aspects that are relevant for the environmental, economic and social impact of food production and consumption have to be included a meaningful definition of sustainable food consumption.

Another new aspect was added to the second part of the study, which focuses on consumers, their attitudes and patterns of food consumption. Based on in-depth qualitative interviews conducted in 2010, consumers are grouped into tentative target groups for promoting sustainable food consumption and for marketing organic food in particular. The classification is based on criteria taken from lifestyle concepts and is focused on the field of food and sustainability. This grouping can provide the basis for further analysis of food-related lifestyle segments and target groups as well as the socio-cultural contexts and implications of middle class food consumption. In terms of empirical data, an additional small quantitative survey was conducted among biology students at a college in Secunderabad to expand the data basis for the assessment of awareness of organic food.

While in many Western countries, sustainable consumption has become a popular and widely discussed topic in academia, public discourses and on the policy agenda, it has as yet received little attention in developing country contexts. In India, organic and fair-trade are tiny niche markets, but they have considerable growth potential. To date, very little in-depth information is available on consumer attitudes and purchasing behaviour of buyers of organic food in India. Apart from the overview provided by (Rao et al. 2006), no comprehensive and in-depth study on the market for organic food in the emerging megacity of Hyderabad has been conducted yet. This study focuses on consumption of products from sustainable agriculture. The overall objective is to give an overview of market structures, examine the role of products from sustainable agriculture in the urban food system and explore new marketing opportunities with a view to their overall sustainability and in particular their climate impact. The focus is on the marketing and consumption stage; differences in production system are only considered as a background for estimating a product's footprint in that stage of the life cycle.

Specific objectives are:

- to explore how sustainable food consumption can be defined in the Indian context, and to explore the role of organic food in a sustainable food system
- to inventorise and map different retail formats selling products from sustainable agriculture across Hyderabad and Secunderabad and to compare them with regard to their sustainability impact
- to assess awareness of and knowledge about organic food among consumers, to investigate their purchasing motivations and obstacles preventing consumers from buying (more) organic products
- to establish preliminary consumer target groups on the basis of their food consumption patterns, food-related values and attitudes, and awareness of the interrelations between food consumption and the environment, particularly climate change
- to explore new marketing opportunities for organic food and make recommendations for action for local stakeholders on how to promote sustainable food consumption

The framework of analysis, presented in Chapter 2, is constituted by the current state of research on assessing the sustainability of food production and consumption, in particular the climate impact of different farming systems, supply chain organisation, retailing formats and consumption patterns. It sets the framework for assessing the research findings on market structures, supply chains, consumer profiles and consumption patterns with regard to sustainability. Chapter 3 outlines the research methodology used for the empirical case study. Chapter 4 provides an overview of the existing market for organic food and a comparative analysis of retail formats with regard to their product availability, price levels, customer profile, suppliers and supply chain organisation. The paper then proceeds to discussing patterns of consumption of organic food in Hyderabad, in particular the socio-economic differentiation of consumers with regard to their awareness of organic food as well as their food purchasing preferences. Motivations as well as constraints for buying organic products are discussed in order to draw conclusions for potential new marketing opportunities for organic food and for strategies for promoting sustainable consumption in general. Chapter 6 compares different retail formats with regard to their feasibility for marketing organic products and assesses their future prospects of growth. Based on the findings, recommendations for developing the urban market for organic food in a sustainable manner are developed. The final chapter also outlines further research areas regarding the role of organic production as well as consumer behaviour in a sustainable urban food system.

# 2 Conceptual and Analytical Framework

## 2.1 Sustainable Consumption: Definitions and Measurements

Sustainability in general refers to the use of any system such as global ecosystems in such a way that its capacity to reproduce itself will not be destroyed in the long run. With regard to human life on earth, this means using the natural resource base without destroying the basis of livelihood of future generations. By now there seems to be widespread consensus that current global systems of production and consumption are not sustainable, that "current unsustainable patterns of production and consumption must be changed" (UN 2000: Millennium Declaration). However, it is far less easy to reach a globally valid and acceptable definition of which consumption patterns would be sustainable. Many contested definitions of sustainable consumption have been developed by different organisations (Jackson 2006). They differ in the extent to which they demand a change in consumption patterns, and in their setting of priorities. Sustainability is very much a political issue that concerns issues of lifestyle choices, social inequality and power.

In recent years, the term sustainability has been applied to a wide and increasing range of topics. On the one hand, this indicates that considerations of sustainability play an increasing role in consumer markets and on the policy level. On the other hand, the concept of sustainability is sometimes being criticised for having become meaningless, because it is employed in such an inflationary and reductionist way. For example, advocates of neoliberal market ideologies tend to reduce sustainability to its economic dimension. A holistic definition of sustainability requires that all dimensions—ecological, economic and social sustainability—are considered equally and simultaneously. It has to address the impact of human actions on both natural ecosystems and human society.

This multidimensional nature of the concept of sustainability calls for a correspondingly complex concept of consumption. Brunner (2009) conceptualises consumption as a dynamic, multi-level process that starts with the emergence of needs and desires, comprises gathering of information about products, purchasing decisions and acts of purchasing, use and transformation (for example by way of cooking) of goods and services and goes all the way to waste disposal. Consumption is not an isolated, individual act but is embedded in a social framework of relationships and trends in society, and it is dependent upon everyday contexts such as household and market structures. Consumption is a specific type of social practice, which is often enacted in routines. In addition to satisfying basic needs such as eating, consumption also serves to express identity, group affiliations or social distinction (cf. Bourdieu 2002; Pütz and Schröder 2006).

As a result of these social functions of consumption, people tend to consume many products beyond their needs. Capitalist production systems exploit this tendency in order to continuously develop and market new products, thus continuously expanding global resource use for consumption purposes. This has lead to many challenges from climate change to soil degradation or social inequality. While the need for more sustainable patterns of production and consumption is widely recognised, the assessment of the sustainability of specific products or consumption patterns requires adequate assessment tools, indicators and measurements. Among the tools that allow for such an assessment are the ecological footprint, product life-cycle assessment and product labels based on specific standards of production. An ecological footprint is an aggregated indicator of the demand of human consumption on the natural resource base (see for example Wackernagel and Rees 1996; Barrett et al. 2005; Collins, Flynn, and Netherwood 2005; Venetoulis and Talberth 2008). It can be calculated for regions, groups of people or individuals. The latter is a measurement for the climate impact of a product. Life-cycle analyses are a tool for calculating the environmental impact of a product across its life-cycle from production, distribution and consumption to disposal.

In addition to the overall ecological footprint, it is also possible to calculate more specific footprints such as water or carbon footprints. In some countries, carbon and climate footprint labels are available for specific products to communicate the product footprint to consumers as a basis for responsible purchasing decisions (Asan 2008). An example of a label awarded to products with a low carbon footprint across their product lifecycle is the Swiss initiative climatop[2] awarding the green "approved by climatop" label to the product with the lowest climate impact of all competitors in the same category. The assessment of the climate impact is based on a life-cycle analysis done by independent agencies. The label is currently in a pilot phase, it will be expanded to include other environmental factors than climate impact as well (ecological footprint rather than just a climate footprint). Another example is the Carbon Reduction Label by the Carbon Trust[3] in the UK. The British Standards Institution also developed a product carbon footprinting standard, the PAS 2050, which "provides a method for assessing the greenhouse gas emissions arising from products across their life cycle, from initial sourcing of raw materials through manufacture, transport, use and ultimately recycling or waste."[4]

While the primary focus of footprint calculations is environmental impact, it also has a strong social dimension in that it expresses social inequalities. The unsustainable overuse of resources by part of the world's population is only possible to the disadvantage of other groups of people as well as future generations. For example, the average footprint per person in Germany is 4.2 global hectares, compared to only 0.9 global hectares for India (WWF 2008). Of course, similar inequalities exist between different social groups within countries. A new development in lifecycle analysis is the emergence of tools for assessing the social impact of production. One such approach for social lifecycle-assessment was developed by the UN Environmental Programme (Benoît and Mazijn 2009). Social product labels such as Fairtrade have focussed on the social conditions of production of agricultural products in developing countries for a long time. They guarantee that the conditions of production conform to certain minimum standards such as working hours, social security, payment and the like.

One of the key points of sustainable consumption is food and nutrition (Bilharz 2009; Bilharz 2007). According to Collins and Fairchild (2007), diet is responsible for around one fourth of the total ecological footprint of individuals. In the US, the food industry consumes nearly one fifth of total petroleum consumed. In order to produce one calorie of food and get it to the consumer's plate, it takes seven to ten calories of fossil fuel energy (Pollan 2006). As both sustainability and consumption have strong socio-economic and socio-cultural implications, there can be no universally valid definition of sustainable consumption. The following sections outline a number of aspects relevant with regard to

---

[2] see www.climatop.ch
[3] see www.carbontrust.co.uk
[4] www.carbontrust.co.uk/carbon/briefing/pre-measurement.htm

the sustainability of food consumption and production in the Indian context. It addresses several factors along the value chain of food products from sustainable agriculture and different systems of distribution and retailing to end consumption ("from farm to fork"). Different approaches for assessing sustainability are presented, many of which take an interdisciplinary approach for analysing sustainability in its environmental, economic and social dimensions.

## 2.2 Sustainable Agriculture

Food production is a vital component of a food system, and hence sustainable farming systems are the point of departure for sustainable food systems. A number of farming systems and techniques can be subsumed under the umbrella of sustainable agriculture. The most basic definition of organic agriculture is growing crops without chemical pesticides and synthetic fertilisers and without genetically modified organisms. Organic livestock is fed on organically grown fodder and reared without the use of antibiotics or growth hormones. In organic food processing, no ionising radiations and food additives or growth promoters are allowed. More than an inventory of techniques, however, organic agriculture was originally intended as a holistic and systemic approach to agriculture:

> *Organic agriculture is a production system that sustains the health of soils, ecosystems and people. It relies on ecological processes, biodiversity and cycles adapted to local conditions, rather than the use of inputs with adverse effects. Organic agriculture combines tradition, innovation and science to benefit the shared environment and promote fair relationships and a good quality of life for all involved.* (Definition by IFOAM, www.ifoam.org/growing_organic/definitions/doa/)

Most countries have policies that regulate and standardise which farming techniques are considered organic. In India, a national organic standard and certification scheme was only established in recent years[5]. Therefore other, non-regulated sustainable agriculture systems, many of which consist of traditional and locally adapted techniques, play an important role in the country.

Another sustainable agriculture system that is popular in India is NPM, which eliminates the use of synthetic pesticides. The aim of NPM is not necessarily to get into

---

[5] See Chapter 4.2 about the Indian organic standard and certification schemes.

organic production, but primarily zero pesticide-exposure for farmers. The prime concern is their health. Instead of synthetic pesticides, NPM relies on home-made concoctions made from neem, garlic, chillies, plant and herb extracts, cow dung and cow urine. These are used along with pheromone traps and other traditional methods of pest control (Misra 2009). Synthetic pesticides are the costliest input in agriculture, so NPM helps farmers cut costs while the yields stay the same and crops fetch better prices.

In addition to organic farming and NPM, a number of other farming systems are connected with greater sustainability than prevailing ones. "These include biodynamic, community-based, eco-agriculture, ecological, environmentally sensitive, extensive, farm-fresh, free-range, low-input, (... or) permaculture. There is a continuing and intense debate about whether agricultural systems using some of these practices can qualify as sustainable." (UNEP/ UNCTAD 2008: 6). While integrated farming systems do not have the strict standards of organic or NPM, they can greatly reduce the need for potentially harmful synthetic inputs. Integrated farming systems take different approaches for integrating livestock and crop production. These include Integrated Farming Systems such Integrated Nutrient Management (INM), Integrated Pest and Disease Management (IPDM) and Integrated Weed Management (IWM). INM, for example, combines "balanced and judicious use of chemical fertilisers, biofertilisers and locally available organic manures like farmyard manure, compost [...] and green manure to maintain soil health and its productivity"[6]. Integrated pest management is based on the principle that in a healthy farm system pests need to be managed rather than disruptively destroyed (see for example Prasad 2008). NPM and Integrated Farming Systems are sometimes seen as a compromise between organic farming and intensive conventional agriculture, or as a temporary stage for farms that are in conversion to organic. In this paper, the term "organic food" is used as comprising both certified organic production and NPM if monitored by NGOs, third-party laboratory tests or operating under a Participatory Guarantee System.

What all of these cultivation systems have in common, to varying degrees, is a better environmental, economic and social performance than conventional farming, particularly in India whose agriculture sector is dominated by resource-poor smallholder producers. Firstly, growing food organically has many benefits for soils, water and biodiversity. "Green revolution technology [...] has been very successful in achieving spectacular results in food grain production during the last three decades. However, signs of fatigue in the natural resources have already emerged and have unleashed various agro-ecological

---

[6] http://india.gov.in/sectors/agriculture/fertilizers.php

problems. It has badly damaged the natural resource base of the country." (Singh 2004: 1) Organic agriculture on the other hand improves soil fertility and soil properties such as microbial biomass, microbial enzyme activities, abundance of earthworms and insects, increased soil aggregate stability, water content and water holding capacity. A global-level comparative analysis of different studies revealed that on organic farms species diversity is 30 % higher and there are 50 % more beneficial animals such as bees and other insects (Niggli 2010). Overall, sustainable agriculture strengthens ecosystem linkages and promotes the healthy functioning of ecosystems. It maintains natural ecosystem services, which are benefits provided to humans by ecosystems. For example, biodiversity provides services such as nutrient cycling, pest regulation and pollination. Many of these ecosystem services ensure the resilience of agriculture and sustain agricultural productivity.

Secondly, sustainable agriculture can significantly reduce fossil fuel consumption and make an important contribution to climate change mitigation and adaptation. Agriculture and diet are among the main contributors to emissions of the greenhouse gases methane, nitrous oxide and carbon dioxide: In the 1990s, approximately 15 % of greenhouse gas emissions globally have been due to agricultural land use (Cole et al. 1997), and most of the global nitrous oxide emissions as well as roughly two thirds of methane emissions originate from agriculture (Kotschi and Müller-Sämann 2004). Agriculture could be an important factor for mitigating climate change. However, "mainstream agriculture is moving in an opposite direction; increasing releases of greenhouse gases from the green sector have made agriculture a producer of global warming rather than a mitigating factor" (Kotschi and Müller-Sämann 2004: 7).

The study by Kotschi and Müller-Sämann (2004) discusses the potential of organic agriculture to avoid and to sequester greenhouse gases, and makes comparisons with conventional agriculture. It clearly states that organic agriculture contributes significantly to the reduction of greenhouse gas releases[7] and to carbon sequestration. Carbon dioxide exists in relatively high concentrations and thus contributes most to global warming. Fossil fuel consumption is a major source of carbon dioxide emissions in agriculture. On average, organic farming has a 30–70 % lower overall energy consumption per unit of land as it uses significantly less fossil fuel than conventional agriculture, and in most cases has a more favourable energy balance. Conventional farming consumes more fossil fuel, for example for the production and transportation of synthetic inputs and for farm

---

[7] For an overview of direct and indirect reduction on agricultural greenhouse gas emissions arising from the principles of Organic Agriculture see Kotschi and Müller-Sämann (2004): page 37, Table 14.

machinery, whereas organic farmers rely primarily on renewable resources and on-farm inputs such as compost, manure and bio-pesticides. External animal feeds are reduced to a minimum and less agricultural machinery is used. Organic farming relies mainly on alternative strategies of maintaining soil fertility and fighting pests such as crop rotation, crop diversification, legume cultivation and mechanical pest control. Another opportunity for reducing carbon dioxide emissions in organic farming is the use of biomass as a substitute for fossil fuel.

Emissions of methane and nitrous oxide are also lower in organic farming. Methane originates mostly from livestock farming, and in tropical countries from wetlands and paddy cultivation. Limited animal stocking rates and limited application of animal manure as well as changes in livestock diet reduce emissions of both methane and nitrous oxides in organic farming. A major part of global gross nitrous oxide emissions stem from soils, mainly from mineral and organic nitrogen fertilisers or nitrogen fixed by legumes. With the massive increase in the application of synthetic nitrogen fertiliser, nitrous oxide levels have dramatically increased as well. As a result, nitrous oxide emission even partly offset reductions in carbon dioxide emissions. Nitrous oxide emission are reduced in organic agriculture because no synthetic nitrogen fertiliser is used, avoiding emission during the energy-intensive process of fertiliser production. Tight nutrient cycles also minimise nitrogen losses. For more details on the climate impact of different farming systems, see for example Niggli et al. (2009); Niggli and Fließbach (2009); Foodwatch (2008); Koerber and Kretschmer (2009); von Koerber et al. (2009).

In addition to its potential for reducing greenhouse gas emissions, organic farming also has great potential for sequestration of carbon in soils and biomass. This is achieved by following the principle of tight nutrient and energy cycles, improved practices in cropland management and agroforestry and through organic matter management in soils. Through long and diversified crop rotations and legume cropping and by regularly adding organic materials to the soil in the form of organic manures and compost it helps maintain or even increase soil organic carbon (Kotschi and Müller-Sämann 2004). With regard to climate change adaptation, sustainable agriculture has great potential as it can reduce water input for fertiliser application and make crops more drought tolerant. Organic farmers also tend to rely more on traditional crops, such as millets in Western Andhra Pradesh, which are more adapted to the local agro-climatic conditions.

Thirdly, in addition to its environmental benefits, organically grown food is also beneficial to the health of producers as well as consumers. Organic farming eliminates the exposure of farmers to harmful chemicals, which cause thousands of deaths and illnesses among Indian farmers each year (Rao et al. 2005; Prabu 2009). It also reduces the risk of contamination with chemical residues in food products. A study conducted in 1996 by the Indian Council of Medical Research found that 51 % of all analysed food items were contaminated with pesticide residues, 20 % even above tolerance levels (Lohr and Dittrich 2007). India is among the countries with the highest levels of toxic residues in food[8] in the world (Chander 1997). In addition to the adverse effects of synthetic inputs, there are also comparative studies that suggest that organic food is nutritionally superior. Organic food has been found to contain more vitamins and micronutrients such as polyphenoles and antioxidants than conventional products grown under the same conditions (Niggli et al. 2007 and www.quilf.org).

Fourthly, organic farming is economically more viable, especially in countries like India where the majority of farms are small and resource-poor. Small organic farms also tend to have a lower level of technology, thus using less energy as well as creating more labour (Singh 2004). Organic farming has a high cost-effectiveness, and even though yields may be smaller than in conventional agriculture for some crops and farming sites, the total average yield and the net profit for farmers are higher in the long run[9] (J. Singh 2004; cf. Eyhorn 2005; Pollan 2006). Niggli (2010) quotes studies that have shown that 100 % conversion to organic farming would impact yields negatively by minus 20–40 % in intensively farmed regions under best geo-climatic conditions, and by up to minus 20 % in less favourable regions. However, he also cites a comparative survey of 200 case studies (UNEP/ UNCTAD 2008) that found a 116 % increase in yields in the context of subsistence agriculture and in regions with periodic disruptions of water supply through droughts and floods.

Smallholder producers in developing countries are at great risk because of their dependence on agrochemical corporations. In India, many small farmers are increasingly indebted due to loans they take for hybrid and genetically-modified seeds, chemical pesticides and fertiliser. As a result, nearly 200,000 farmers have committed suicide in India over the last ten years. The comprehensive study by UNEP and UNCTAD (2008) shows for the African context how different locally adapted sustainable agriculture systems contribute to improvements in food security.

---

[8] Cf. Ramanjaneyulu and Chennamaneni (2007) for an analysis of the institutional context of pesticide regulation in India, with special reference to vegetables in Hyderabad market.

[9] The experts interviewed for this study generally agreed that the yields can be higher in organic farming for some crops, for example for leafy vegetables, and that overall they are almost equal to conventional farming.

An analysis based on case studies of different farming systems concluded that organic farming systems are superior to conventional agriculture both in terms of their productivity and their sustainability. For a concise but comprehensive overview of the advantages of sustainable agriculture over conventional, growth-oriented agriculture see J. Singh (2004: 281-3). While organic farming is not the only sustainable farming system, it is "unique in the sense that it offers a strategy which systematically integrates most of them in a farming system" (Kotschi and Müller-Sämann 2004: 9). It also has the advantage of reliability and transparency since it operates with compulsory standards well-functioning mechanisms of inspection and certification guaranteeing compliance with organic principles and standards. Conversely, it is not necessarily the case that organic farming is more sustainable than other farming systems in every respect. The scale of the farming system, the degree of mechanisation and the complexity of the supply chain all have an impact on energy consumption and emission levels. In India, a 10–20 % increase in yield achieved by mechanization would cost an extra 43–260 % in energy consumption (Pretty 1995, cited in Kotschi and Müller-Sämann 2004). Pollan (2006) shows for the US that organic food produced on an industrial scale has an equal or in some cases even worse ecological footprint than conventional food.

## 2.3 Diet and Food Choices

More than the type and scale of the farming system, the overall ecological footprint of a food product is determined to a large degree by the type of food item[10] (Collins and Fairchild 2007). In general, animal products have a much higher environmental impact than products of plant origin, meat and fish making up the biggest share. The type of meat also makes a significant difference, cattle having the highest impact and chicken the lowest. For agricultural products, cultivation for crops or rearing for livestock is usually the stage in the product life-cycle with the highest energy use, carbon emission and overall environmental impact, for example due to water consumption and pollution of soils and water (Asan 2008).

In India, the case of livestock farming is somewhat different to other regions. A larger part of the population is vegetarian, either out of religious reasons or because they cannot afford animal products. Further, chicken and mutton are much more common than beef which has the biggest climate impact. In terms of its strong vegetarian tradition, India can thus be seen to have a certain lead in terms of sustainable food consumption, which

---

[10] For an overview on the footprint of different items see Collins and Fairchild (2007) for Cardiff, or www.steppingforward.org.uk/ef/food.htm for the Southwest of England.

is inherent in its food culture. However, dairy products are an integral part of many people's diet, and non-vegetarian Indians do eat considerable amounts of meat. Furthermore, the food culture and consumption patterns are changing rapidly (cf. Hofmann and Dittrich 2009), and meat consumption is on the rise particularly among the affluent urban milieus who often function as role models for lower socio-economic groups. Dairy and poultry farming on large, industrial scales are thus becoming increasingly common.

In addition to carbon dioxide, methane is another greenhouse gas that contributes significantly to global warming. Sources and emission levels of methane differ across geographical regions and depend on the level of agricultural intensification. In Western Europe, 17 % of methane emissions are caused by animal dung and one third by application of semi-liquid manure. In tropical countries, the most important sources of methane emissions are paddy fields and wetlands, which together make up around one third of global gross emissions of methane (Kotschi and Müller-Sämann 2004). In India, ruminant livestock farming does not play as significant a role as in other parts of the world, but a trend towards more industrialised patterns of dairy farming and poultry raising is emerging. Organic livestock farming considerably reduces methane emissions due to changes in ruminant diet.

## 2.4 Supply Chains and Regional Food Networks

According to figures cited by Pollan (2006), only one fifth of the total energy consumption of a food product is consumed on the farm, whereas the rest is used for processing and transport. A major part of the energy consumed in the life-cycle of a food product is used for processing. The higher the level of processing, the more energy-intensive the product becomes. For ready-to-eat, prewashed and packaged organic lettuce in a US supermarket, it takes more than 57 calories of fossil fuel energy per calorie of food. The figures would only be about 4 % higher if the lettuce was grown conventionally. Of course, these figures cannot be taken as representative for India, but there too the tendency towards more highly processed foods is visible throughout urban retail markets. In addition to energy consumption, processed food also tends to be packaged more, thus contributing to urban waste disposal problems.

The concept of food miles refers to the distance over which a product is being transported in the course of its production and distribution. It appears rather obvious that the more local the origin of a product the more environmentally friendly it is. However, recent studies have found that food miles do not in fact constitute the major part of the carbon footprint, and even less so on the overall ecological footprint of a food product compared to the production stage (DeWeerdt 2009). For the food system of Cardiff, UK, for example, Collins and Fairchild (2007) calculated that it only makes up 1.7% of the total footprint. Of course, such figures for other regions cannot be transferred directly to the Indian context, as average distances, transport infrastructure and energy use of vehicles is widely different. Even though food miles are only one factor among many in the total ecological footprint of a product, they are nevertheless relevant for the overall product carbon footprint, particularly when comparing the performance of different supply chain models for the same product.

Organic farming plays a vital role in the regionalisation of supply chains and strengthening of local food systems. Supply chains tend to be shorter, organic products usually are less processed, their cultivation is less resource intensive and it supports the local economy by creating more employment and sourcing its inputs locally. Increasingly popular systems of marketing and distribution that are associated with local food systems include community-organised agriculture[11] initiatives, box delivery schemes and the like, which aim to establish more direct linkages between producers and consumers. While in the US the local food movement is very strong (see Wikipedia 2009), in India such initiatives are still rare but becoming increasingly popular too. A successful example of an organic box delivery scheme near Pune is described by Dharmadhikary (2010), and the Sahaja Aharam Organic Consumer Cooperative is portrayed in Chapter 4.4 as a local example in Hyderabad. In addition to food miles and freshness of produce, another benefit of local food systems are closer links between producers and consumers. These encourage transparency of production and accountability of producers. Furthermore, a local food system is best suited for supplying local crops that are best adapted to the ecological conditions, the traditional farming systems and local food culture.

In addition to food miles and regionalisation, an analysis of the footprint of a food product from farm to plate also has to take into account the final stages of the supply chain. Different retail formats differ significantly with regard to their energy consumption, for example large malls and supermarkets with their lighting, air-conditioning and cold storage facilities will have a significantly higher impact than farmer's markets or street vendors that do not even use electricity. However, if consumers regularly visit local farmers by car, the emissions contribute a major share to the overall footprint of the product. Therefore, the final stage of the supply chain, transport from the retailer to the end consumer, also has to figure in a life-cycle assessment.

---

[11] These projects are especially popular in the US. Of course their overall environmental impact may in fact be higher than in conventional farming and retailing, given that many consumers travel to their community farm every weekend by car and thus offset the fossil fuel savings of organic farming.

## 2.5 Lifestyle and Consumer Behaviour

The previous sections indicated that individual consumption patterns and consumer behaviour play an important role for sustainable consumption. Lifestyle concepts are one approach for consumer segmentation and identification of target groups, which has been variously applied for example in sociology, social ecology and market research. "Lifestyles are group specific forms of how individuals live and interpret their lives in a social context. (...) Lifestyles link social structure to attitude and behaviour. The lifestyle perspective (...) reveals the socio-cultural plurality of societies." (Reusswig, Lotze-Campen, and Gerlinger 2005: 198) There is no consistent definition, methodology or empirical operationalisation of the lifestyle concept. Three core dimensions are usually used to construct lifestyle groups: social status, attitudes and preferences, which together are often referred to as 'mentality', and behaviour. While lifestyle concepts are useful for identifying target groups, they have some limitations when it comes to explaining consumer behaviour and an in-depth academic inquiry of socio-cultural meanings of consumption patterns. Nevertheless, Reusswig, Lotze-Campen, and Gerlinger (2005: 198) argue that the approach has great value beyond its uses for consumer segmentation because "lifestyles and lifestyle changes [can also be seen] as drivers of social change —something to be kept in mind with regard to the sustainability transition. People are not only consumers, they are ethical persons and political actors at the same time".

To date, the lifestyle concept has not been very frequently employed for analysing sustainable consumption. Enneking, Franz, and Profeta (2007) argue that the interlinkages between consumption and sustainability need to be analysed context-specifically, i.e. for example for the fields of mobility, housing, or food and nutrition. There are several reasons for this. Sustainable consumption patterns in one field, for example mobility, do not necessarily coincide with sustainable practices in another field, for example food consumption. Further, people's consumption behaviour these days is often strongly hybrid and depends on many factors like time constraints, financial budget, individual preferences or availability. This makes it hard to generalise across different fields.

Two models for a segmentation of consumers in Germany into lifestyle segments specifically for the field of food and nutrition are presented here. They partly informed the tentative segmentation into organic target groups in Chapter 5.4. The first one is the food-related lifestyle segmentation developed by the German Institute of Social-Ecological Research (Hayn 2005; Stieß and Hayn 2005; Götz 2001). It distinguishes seven groups who are categorised by three core dimensions: orientations, which comprises values, attitudes and preferences in relation to overall lifestyle as well as the specific field of action (here: food); social status, which includes socio-demographic and socio-economic factors; and field-specific behaviour. Most of the food-related lifestyle groups they distinguish can be associated with a specific biographical phase, for example the group of "conventional health-oriented" consumers is predominant in the post-family and early retirement phase, whereas the "fitness-oriented ambitious" consumers are mostly young singles or couples without or with young children (Stieß and Hayn 2005).

A second, more specifically sustainability-focused segmentation of food-related lifestyles was developed by Enneking, Franz, and Profeta (2007). They derive five "sustainability segments" or "sustainability milieus" based on criteria that relate to sustainability of food consumption, viz. consumption of organic products, meat consumption, use of frozen foods, as well as aspects of food-related mentality regarding these variables. In addition to these constituent variables other aspects such as eating out, general lifestyle characteristics and socio-economic status were used to characterise the five segments. For each variable, actual behaviour was inquired in terms of frequency of consumption for organic food, meat, frozen foods, eating out and cooking at home. In addition, food-related mentality was assessed on the basis of questions relating to perceptions of the sustainability of organic food production, meat consumption and frozen foods consumption as well as the importance for individual food consumption lifestyle. A representative sample survey that was analysed using a two-step cluster analysis resulted in five distinct "sustainability segments": anti-organic meat eaters, convenience-oriented consumers, frequent organic buyers, and occasional organic buyers[12] (Enneking, Franz, and Profeta 2007). These five segments have an almost equal share of one fifth of the German population.

Such food lifestyle segments developed in other regional settings cannot be applied unmodified to the Indian context. Not only is the food availability very different, but more importantly the socio-cultural meanings and practices associated with food. Context-specific constituent variables need to be developed that adequately represent and take into account those aspects that are most relevant with regard to sustainable food consumption in the Indian context. The present study looks at lifestyle groups specifically for the field of food and nutrition in its intersections with sustainability issues. It develops a tentative target group segmentation for sustainable food consumption in Hyderabad[13], based on variables of food consumption behaviour (purchasing of organic food, vegetarianism), food- and sustainability-related attitudes and values (health-

---

[12] My translations, the original names are: "Öko-misstrauische Fleischliebhaber", "Wenig-Fleisch-Esser", "Convenience-Betonte", "Intensive Ökokäufer", "Leichte Ökokäufer".
[13] See Chapter 5.4.

consciousness, environmental-consciousness, food preferences) and socio-economic and socio-demographic variables (education, profession, income, experience abroad, age, family status).

Together with socio-economic status and mentality, behaviour is an important constituent of lifestyle. In the social sciences, analyses of human behaviour are often based on Bourdieu's theory of practice. The French sociologist Pierre Bourdieu explored social patterns of consumption in his 1984 publication Distinction: A Social Critique of the Judgement of Taste. He found that taste for a wide range of cultural goods, including food, is determined primarily by family socialisation processes and educational experiences. He found that consumption choices are not simply personal and socially inconsequential, but that social status can be gained, lost and reproduced in part through everyday acts of consumption. Bourdieu shows why consumer goods can contain a lot more meaning than their mere practical value would suggest. The cultural meanings of food include symbolic values of certain goods or consumption practices and can be located in the socio-economic, religious or other spheres. This is where the influence of the media and advertising comes in, as has great power to shape preferences and evoke new wishes. For consumers that are beyond daily concerns about basic food security, a significant financial and time effort goes into pursuing food consumption that has nothing to do with their need for nutrition. Bourdieu also showed that the symbolic values of consumption practices play an important part in establishing and maintaining basic structures of power and social inequality.

The relatively young field of behavioural economics, a social science branch in economics, investigates why people make certain choices, often despite better knowledge that a different choice would have more benefits in the long run. For example, Thaler and Sunstein (2009) do research on choice architecture and advocate the concept of libertarian paternalism, which allows choice architects to "nudge" people to make more sustainable choices without actually limiting their individual freedom of choice. Thaler and Sunstein investigate why people who are environmentally conscious do not behave in a corresponding, ecological manner. One obvious reason is a lack of knowledge of environmental consequences of our behaviour. But even where people are aware of the consequences, they may still choose to ignore their knowledge and choose the easiest way. According to Thaler and Sunstein, convenience is a major factor determining our behaviour. The trend towards increasing consumption of convenience products and fast food that has been observed the urban Indian middle classes in recent years (Lohr and

Dittrich 2007) gives rise to the assumption that this is no different in India than in the US, where Thaler and Sunstein developed their theory.

Consumer behaviour like shopping habits, food choices and food preparation is determined by various intrinsic and extrinsic factors like individual preferences, socialisation in a particular food culture, personal contexts, infrastructure and product availability. Individual purchasing decisions are determined not only by cultural and symbolic functions but also by structures such as access to food and infrastructure (for example, purchasing power, availability of certain products, accessibility of outlets and convenience, information about products and outlets). These structures can either facilitate or obstruct sustainable food choices. Supply and demand can be seen as mutually dependent; consumption patterns are neither determined by structures alone, nor are they an accumulation of entirely free and independent consumer choices (Brand 2008). For a comprehensive analysis of food consumption patterns, an approach is needed that takes into account both individual practices of food consumption and the institutional and structural context, which shapes and is shaped by these practices. Why do some consumers who are aware of and have a positive attitude towards organic food still not buy it? Analysing existing knowledge-behaviour gaps and investigating the context-specific reasons can help identify obstacles that arise either from market structures and availability or from consumer needs and preferences, or both. Bogun 2008) argues that an analysis of knowledge-behaviour gaps in the field of sustainable consumption should view environmental and social consequences as risks. Consumption choices thus become ways of negotiating these risks.

# 3 Research Methodology

## 3.1 Definitions and Consumer Classification

One of the most important premises for conducting this survey was a clear conception of "organic food". A good deal of confusion was found to exist among consumers and even some experts about the meaning of "organic"[14]. In order to ascertain that respondents have a clear understanding of the terminology used in the survey, consumers that reported to be aware of organic food were asked to give a brief definition. The minimum reply that was taken to indicate at least a basic understanding of the concept was "farming without chemicals".

---

[14] See Chapter 2.2 for a definition of "organic" and how the term is used in this paper; see Chapter 5 for common misconceptions about organic food among survey respondents.

Another important concern was how to classify consumers and potential new consumers of sustainable food products. Chakrabarti and Baisya (2007) classify buyers according to regularity of purchase: regular buyers spend more than 75 % of expenditure on organic food in a food category, and occasional buyers 25–75 %. This classification was found not to be practical, because regularity refers more to a frequency than a percentage, and many consumers are not able to estimate the share of organic food in their total food expenditures per food category at all. Therefore an attempt was made to assess regularity by asking consumers about the frequency of buying each organic food category per week or month. In German-language research on organic food consumptions, buyers are usually similarly grouped into regular, occasional and non-buyers[15]. In order to assess the relative importance of organic food consumption, they were also asked whether organic products make up more or less than 50 % of their expenditure in a food category. However, due to the low availability of organic food in Hyderabad, the distinction was not found to be very relevant. At this stage, the vast majority of organic consumers are inevitably occasional buyers for most food items, simply due to the limited availability of organic products.

## 3.2 Primary Data Collection

One part of this survey comprised a total of 144 concise, structured quantitative interviews conducted in 2009, and a questionnaire survey with 33 biology master students at a college in Secunderabad conducted in 2010. The objective was to get a broad overview of attitudes and knowledge among different parts of the general population. Interviews covered questions on potential concerns over chemical residues in food products, awareness of organic food, purchasing of organic food and awareness of organic labels. Thirty percent of the respondents in the quantitative survey purchase organic products regularly or occasionally.

A total of 39 longer, semi-structured qualitative consumer interviews aimed at getting more information about the purchasing patterns and motivations of consumers that are aware of organic food. Of those, 18 respondents were female and 21 male. Most of them were in the middle age groups, 16 of them in the age group 20-45 years, and another 16 in the group 46-60 years. Only 7 were over 60 years old. Almost all respondents were responsible for most of the shopping for their households; some shared responsibility with their spouse. Five never buy organic products, 16 occasionally and 18 regularly.

---

[15] "Intensiv-, Gelegenheits- und NichtkäuferInnen", see for example Brunner (2009).

In the second research phase in 2010, a total of 10 unstructured qualitative consumer interviews were conducted with consumers from different backgrounds that already had some level of awareness of and/ or experience with organic food. Respondents were approached through informal networks and organisation such as the Sahaja Aharam Organic Consumer Cooperative, Greenpeace and organic shops. Interviews were conducted as household interviews or in other setting that were convenient for respondents, such as the Sahaja Aharam office. The objective was to gain in-depth insights into their socio-demographic, socio-economic and socio-cultural backgrounds as well as their food habits, values, attitudes and motivations. These interviews also provided the basis for exploring preliminary descriptors for establishing food-related lifestyle segments and assessing the relevance of some preliminary descriptors for developing these segments.

**Table 1:** Semi-structured consumer interviews 2009

| Location | Geographical area and average consumer profile | Quantitative interviews | Qualitative interviews |
| --- | --- | --- | --- |
| Q-Mart | Banjara Hills, predominantly upper and upper middle class | 41 interviews | 6 interviews |
| Spencer's Hyper | Musheerabad, mixed, predominantly middle class | 40 interviews | 5 interviews |
| Batkammakunta slum | Vidyanagar, lower and lower middle class | 11 interviews | none |
| Mehdipatnam Rythu Bazaar | Mehdipatnam, mixed, predominantly middle class | 38 interviews | 5 interviews |
| Vijaya Enterprises | Chikkatpally, mixed, predominantly middle class | 14 interviews | 4 interviews |
| HACA NPM vegetable outlet | Nampally, mixed, predominantly middle class | none | 5 interviews |
| DDS Organic Mobile | Tarnaka, Balkampet and Ramanthapur, mixed, predominantly middle class | none | 10 interviews |
| Brinjal Biodiversity Festival[a] | Hitec City, mixed, predominantly middle class | none | 4 interviews |
| Bhavan's Vivekananda College of Science, Humanities and Commerce | Secunderabad, middle class students aged 21-23 | 33 questionnaires | none |
| Household interviews | several locations, mixed, predominantly middle class | none | 20 interviews |

[a] A food festival organised at the Shilparamam Art Gallery on March 8, 2009 by several local NGOs including CSA and DDS; organic millet was for sale by DDS.

In selecting the locations and interview respondents for both the quantitative and qualitative interviews an effort was made to cover a range of different retail formats selling organic food as well as a broad range of socio-economic customer profiles. Unfortunately, a permission to conduct interviews with customers of the 24-Letter-Mantra store could not be obtained from the store management. Therefore part of the organic consumers[16] in Hyderabad were probably not captured by the survey. The socio-economic properties of the research population indicate that there was a bias among respondents of the qualitative survey towards higher-income, educated groups as well as consumers of organic food as a result of the choice of interview locations. Most respondents in the qualitative survey belonged to the middle classes. Socio-economic categories of consumers used in this study are based on the income categories established by NCAER (2005) (see Table 2). In addition to income, education level (see Table 3), occupation of all income earners and mode of transport used for shopping were used for assessing the socio-economic background of respondents. The average household size was 3.8 and varied between 3 and 4.1 across income groups. The distribution of respondents with regard to level of education was similar to the income groups and overall relatively high. In line with their educational level, most respondents spoke English at an excellent level (27.6 %), or at least well enough to be able to do the interview in English (44.8 %), and less than one third (27.6 %) needed a translation into Telugu or Hindi.

**Table 2:** Semi-structured consumer interviews 2009

| Income category | Estimated total household income per month in INR | Percentage of total respondents |
| --- | --- | --- |
| Category 1 | Less than 90,000 | 3 % |
| Category 2 (lower middle class) | 90,000 to 200,000 | 27 % |
| Category 3 (upper middle class) | 200,000 to 500,000 | 38 % |
| Category 4 (higher middle class) | 500,000 to 1 million | 12 % |
| Category 5 | 1 to 2 million | 12 % |
| Category 6 | More than 2 million | 8 % |

**Table 3:** Education level in the semi-structured interviews

| Education category | Education category | Percentage of total respondents (n = 39) |
| --- | --- | --- |
| Category 1 | Less than high-school degree | 7 % |
| Category 2 | High-school graduate | 10 % |
| Category 3 | Graduate degree | 45 % |
| Category 4 | Postgraduate degree | 35 % |
| Category 5 | Doctorate | 3 % |

[16] The 24-Letter-Mantra management could not provide any figures about the number of customers they reach.

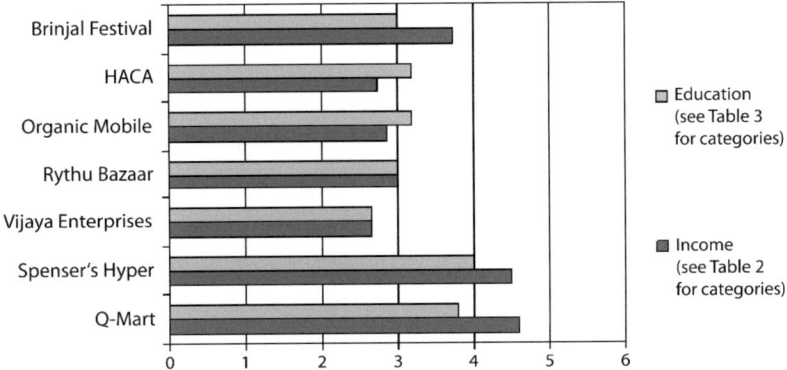

**Figure 1:** Average income and education levels in the semi-structured interviews, compared across interview locations
*Source:* Own data

In addition to consumer interviews, semi-structured and unstructured qualitative interviews were conducted with farmers from cooperatives in rural and peri-urban areas within a radius of 150 km from Hyderabad, in order to get a comprehensive picture of the commodity chains for organic agricultural products that are produced in rural and peri-urban areas around Hyderabad "from farm to fork", or from producer to end consumer. At the marketing stage, farmers selling at Mehdipatnam Rythu Bazaar and the HACA NPM outlet in Hyderabad, retailers and supermarket managers (Q-Mart, Spencer's Hyper, Food Bazaar, 24-Letter-Mantra) were interviewed. In order to get an assessment of the potential for marketing organic products to bulk purchasers of food, several shorter phone interviews with hotel restaurants and canteens were conducted. A number of informational meetings and semi-structured and unstructured interviews with experts from research institutions, NGOs and government organisations working in the field of sustainable agriculture or food and nutrition were conducted on various aspects of organic agriculture, marketing of organic products and the urban food system in general.

Interviews were conducted in English where respondents had a very good command of English, and with the assistance of a translator speaking Hindi and Telugu in the other cases. Both the Hindi and Telugu terms for organic farming[17] were used in addition to the English term in order to avoid misunderstandings.

---

[17] Hindi: Sajeev Kheti, which translates as "living agriculture", "natural farming, or "a way of farming that lays maximum emphasis on regenerating the living soil." (www.imsc.res.in/~nick/kalp_bio.doc); Telugu: Sendriya Vyavasayam.

In addition to interviews, a database of shops selling organic and NPM products in Hyderabad was compiled[18]. For each outlet, photographs were taken, question-led observations made and a survey of availability and price levels of organic products compared to conventional products conducted. Primary data collection furthermore comprised an analysis of the discourses on agriculture, food, nutrition and health in articles in magazines and newspapers.

In the second research phase in 2010, a screening of "I Want My Father Back" by Suma Josson, a film about the agrarian crisis and organic farming in India, was organised. After the film a group discussion provided an opportunity to gain an insight into which topics are important to consumers with regard to food and sustainability, and to gather ideas for promoting sustainable lifestyles. The audience consisted of organic movement activists, aware organic consumers and interested members of the general public. A presentation on organic farming and subsequent discussion was also held at Bhavan's Vivekananda College of Science, Humanities and Commerce subsequent to the student questionnaire survey.

## 3.3 Secondary Data Collection

Research for secondary data and literature was done at the NIN library in Hyderabad and on the Internet. Relevant publications were also gathered from NGOs and experts. Among other publications, findings of the following studies were particularly important as a basis for the survey in Hyderabad:

- "The Market for Organic Foods in India: Consumer Perceptions and Market Potential" (Rao et al. 2006) commissioned by ICCOA in 2006 and covering eight metropolitan cities

- "Purchase Motivations and Attitudes of Organic Food Buyers" (Chakrabarti and Baisya 2007) conducted in the National Capital Region (NCR)

- "Market Opportunities and Challenges for Indian Organic Products" (Garibay and Jyoti 2003) based on a small consumer survey in Mumbai

---

[18] See map Figure 4 and Table 4.

# 4 Sustainable Agriculture: Production and Distribution

## 4.1 Production and Marketing in India

Estimates on how much area is under organic cultivation in India vary widely. According to Bhattacharyya (2004), realistic estimates figure somewhere between 50,000 hectares and 3.5 million hectares. APEDA estimates the area under export-oriented certified organic cultivation at 2.8 million hectares, and ICCOA assumes that 1.2 million hectares or less than 1 % of total cultivable land area are certified organic or under conversion. The area under organic production has been growing steadily over the past years, and more than 714,000 mostly small farmers have registered under certified organic management (Menon et al. 2009).

Often it is not entirely clear whether figures cited in the literature refer to certified organic production only, or include lands under more broadly defined sustainable agriculture production. In many parts of India such as the Himalaya, the Deccan Plateau or the Adivasi area across Central India farmers still practice traditional ways of farming with no or very little external aggro-chemical inputs. According to (Anshu and Mehta n.y.: 1) only one fifth of dry land farmers in India use chemical inputs at all. These production systems can be considered "essentially organic" (Bhattacharyya 2004: 175). While such products cannot actually be marketed as organic, these traditional farming practices nevertheless constitute a huge potential for India's organic sector, because conversion to organic practices is quite easy and, more importantly still, they still have a large pool of knowledge on traditional and sustainable farming methods that have been lost in areas where industrial technology revolutionised farming: "India has a rich heritage of agricultural traditions that are suitable for designing organic production systems." (Garibay and Jyoti 2003).

Apart from farmers' investment capacity and remoteness, the extent to which chemical inputs are used in conventional farming also depends on the type of crops. Pesticide-use is generally high in crops like chillies, leafy vegetables, okra, brinjal and cotton and lower in tuber crops. The regions in Western Andhra Pradesh are mainly drylands with rainfed agriculture and fewer pesticides are applied there compared to the Eastern irrigated farmlands.

## 4.2 Institutional Context and Organic Certification

India's National Agricultural Policy (NAP) launched in 2000 aims to attain "Growth that is sustainable technologically, environmentally and economically." (Government of India 2000) In this context, the National Programme for Organic Production (NPOP) was launched by the Ministry of Commerce. National Standards for Organic Products (NSOP, see Government of India 2005) regulating production, processing, labelling, storage and transport as well as inspection and certification procedures were developed on the basis of guidelines by the IFOAM.

Although the National Horticulture Mission and State Horticulture Mission do support organic horticulture (fruits, vegetables, spices) and vermicompost production to some extent, their programmes do not reach small independent farmers. The Department of Agriculture, Government of India, is not supporting organic production for the domestic market (cf. Richter and Kovacs 2005), only for big farmers that produce for the commercial and export market. The New Agricultural Policy of the Government of India also displays a strong export orientation (J. Singh 2004; Carroll 2005; cf. IBEF 2004). There is no overall strategic attention for greening agriculture[19] (Anshu and Mehta n.y.: 10) or developing the domestic market for organic food. To date, nine Indian states have adopted organic policies, among them Karnataka, Kerala, Uttarakhand, and a few North-Eastern states. Orissa, which does not have an organic policy, produces the highest volumes in certified organic products (Ghosh 2007).

According to DDS, the government supports organic farming on the policy level, but it is not connected to the farm level. At present, most support for small organic farmers with regard to training, extension services, information and marketing assistance is delivered by the NGO sector which is very strong in India (Garibay and Jyoti 2003). However, if the domestic market for organic products is to be developed, policy changes in favour of organic agriculture are urgently needed. "Currently marginal attention is given to the policy framework and institutional dynamics. Involvement of government not just in standardisation and accreditation procedures but also through proactive support to certification and market-oriented services are required." (Anshu and Mehta n.y.: 11)

The fact that NPOP was launched under the control of the Ministry of Commerce is an indication that the government views organic farming mainly as a strategy of capitalising

---

[19] One indication of this is the fact that the website on Organic Farming of the Department of Agriculture and Cooperation, Ministry of Agriculture, Government of India (http://agricoop.nic.in/TaskForce/chep15.htm) was last updated in 2005.

on demand for organic food in other countries through increased export production. Sustainable consumption on the domestic level is not the primary target, nor is the support of small-scale organic farmers and sustainable rural development through organic agriculture. The overview on research funding for modern agriculture given by DDS (2008) clearly indicates that there is a strong bias towards modern, growth-oriented conventional agriculture, in particular biotechnology. This is due to the increasing engagement of aggro-industry corporations in research funding. Many universities in India are funded by agricultural corporations to carry out research, and many government research institutions have entered into agreements and collaborations with private corporations (DDS 2008: 3). There is hardly any funding for research projects or institutions working on sustainable farming practices. The "National Project on Management of Soil Health and Fertility" (NPMSF) of the Government of India supports integrated farming systems development by running soil testing laboratories, conducting fertiliser quality controls and promoting organic manures.

Under the framework of the NPOP, a national organic label (see Figure 2) was developed, and it was stipulated that inspection and certification by one of the nationally accredited certification bodies is mandatory for labelling and selling products as "organic". At present there are six official accreditation agencies in India: APEDA, Coffee Board, Spice Board, Tea Board, Coconut Development Board and Cocoa & Cashew Nut Board. There are also a number of certification agencies accredited under NPOP, for example ECOCERT, IMO, INDOCERT, LACON GmbH, SGS and SKAL.

**Figure 2:** Official India Organic label
*Source:* APEDA

The official India Organic label can be found on organic products exported from India or sold domestically in organic stores and supermarkets. At this stage, it is mainly large-scale operators that are certified with the India Organic label. The fees for organic certification[20] are one of the main obstacles for small farmers applying for the organic label. Garibay and Jyoti (2003) found that the most important constraint stopping farmers from applying for organic certification are the high costs.

In order to provide an alternative for the costly official organic certification schemes for small organic farmers, increasing numbers of rural development NGOs across the world prefer to work with Participatory Guarantee Systems (PGS). These are local-level quality assurance systems certifying producers through a system of participation and peer monitoring. Around the world, a significant number of PGS has evolved as part of the organic agriculture movement. These systems vary in terms of methodology and approach, but they share common principles and values. PGS are often linked to localised and alternative approaches to marketing.

**Figure 3:** PGS (Participatory Guarantee System) Organic label
*Source:* PGS Organic India Council

In India, the PGS India Organic Council developed the PGS Organic label (see Figure 3) in cooperation with the Food and Agricultural Organisation (FAO) and the Ministry of Agriculture, Government of India. This label "certifies sustainably grown organic farm crops that are built on the foundations of quality, trust and alliance through a farmer's social network" (PGS India Organic Council brochure).

## 4.3 Organic Marketing and Retailing in India

Major products produced in India under organic farming are tea, rice, fruits and vegetables, wheat and cotton as well as smaller quantities of coffee, spices, pulses, oil seeds and herbal extracts. Most of these are sold in semi-processed or raw forms (Garibay and Jyoti 2003). The bulk of Indian organic production goes into export markets: About

---

[20] See list of certification fees from INDOCERT: www.indocert.org/services.aspx?id=1 and Garibay and Jyoti 2003.

70 % according to Carroll (2005), and as much as 92.5 % of sales according to Garibay and Jyoti (2003). This is a result of the export-oriented government policies and the fact that world market prices for organic products are about 20–30 % higher than for conventional products (Carroll 2005). Many market analysts, marketers and NGOs expect the demand for organic food within India to rise in the near future. The major markets for organic products are in the metropolitan areas, especially Mumbai, Delhi, Kolkata, Chennai, Bangalore and Hyderabad.

The main obstacles impeding the development of the domestic market for organic food are lack of knowledge about organic farming among farmers, limited and inconsistent supply, inadequate retail presence and an incomplete product range, in-transparent market structures (e.g. price levels), high certification costs and hence lack of certified products, uncompetitive price levels, lack of awareness among consumers, low demand, and government policies that are skewed towards exports (Carroll 2005: 1; Bhattacharyya 2004: 164). Consumer price levels of organic food are still significantly higher than for "conventional" food, and "organic food is priced over 25 % more than conventional food in India" (Organicfacts 2006).

Within the Indian retail market for organic food, there is a continuum of different systems of production and distribution. On the one end of this continuum is what might be called the corporate retail strategy. In Hyderabad, this category is dominated by Sresta Bioproducts and 24-Letter-Mantra organic stores as well as supermarkets selling organic products from different suppliers. These commercial companies usually operate on an India-wide scale and are certified with the India Organic label. According to (Bhattacharyya 2004: 163), these wholesalers and traders have a share of 60 % in the distribution of organic products in the country. At the other end of the continuum are smallholder producers who are often supported in their direct marketing initiatives by local non-profit and rural development NGOs. The two ends of this continuum differ in terms of the farming system, the structure of the supply chain, and the retailing strategy they involve, all of which significantly influence the group of consumers they are targeted at as well as their climate impact. Most domestic-bound organic products are uncertified, because the majority of producers are small or marginal farmers and small cooperatives (Carroll 2005).

## 4.4 Market Structures in Hyderabad

This chapter gives an overview of retailing of organic, natural and health food in Hyderabad and Secunderabad. Organic food is still very much a niche market in India, which is reflected in the limited availability. However, while in 2006, there were only six outlets selling organic products in Hyderabad (Lohr and Dittrich 2007), a significant increase both in the number of retail outlets stocking organic food and in product range could be witnessed over the over the past four years. Table 4 and Figure 4 show the most important organic food outlets in Hyderabad. For several reasons, it was not possible in the scope of this study to provide a complete inventory of organic food retailing for several reasons: The organic market segment is highly dynamic and expanding continuously, and only selected geographic areas were surveyed in this study, so that especially for modern retail formats no city-wide estimate of the number of shops and supermarkets stocking organic food or of their product range could be made. However, it can be safely assumed that the most important outlets are captured by this list. The ensuing subchapters portray the major types of organic outlets in Hyderabad and Secunderabad. More small health food stores and organic retailing businesses might in fact exist across the city, but they are hard to find as their publicity is largely restricted to word of mouth.

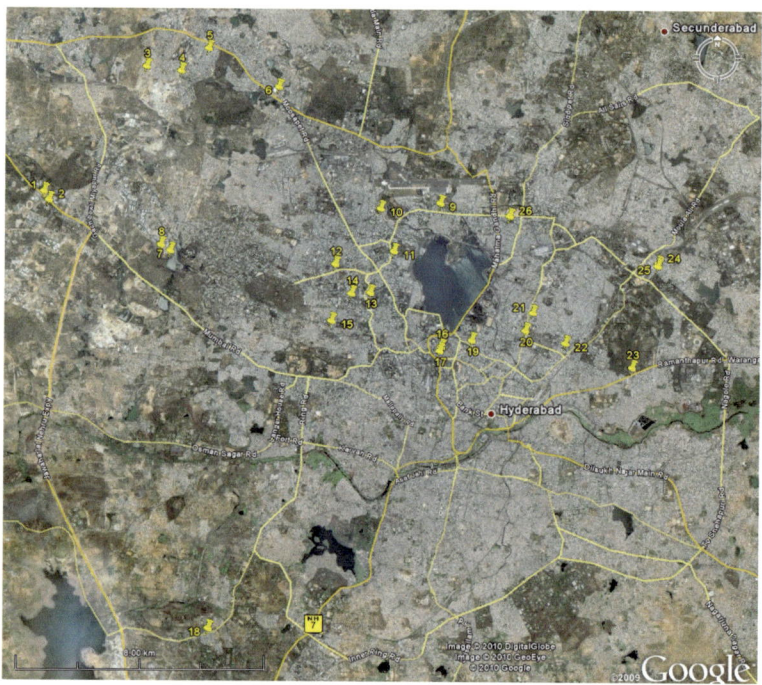

**Figure 4:** Overview map of organic outlets in Hyderabad and Secunderabad (list of outlets see Table 4)

*Source:* Google Earth, own data

**Table 4:** Education level in the semi-structured interviews

| No. in map | Name of store | Neighbourhood | Main suppliers of organic products | Opening days |
|---|---|---|---|---|
| **Supermarkets and hypermarkets** | | | | |
| 7 | Hypercity hypermarket | Inorbit Mall, Hitec City | various | daily |
| 6 | Metro Cash and Carry | Kukatpally | Ecofarms Ltd. | daily |
| 12 | Q-Mart | Banjara Hills | Sresta Bioproducts Ltd. | daily |
| 11 | SPAR | Begumpet | Pro Nature Organic Foods | daily |
| 2 | SPAR | Gachibowli | Pro Nature Organic Foods | daily |
| – | Spencer's supermarkets | Across the city | Sresta Bioproducts Ltd. | daily |
| 21 | Spencer's Hyper | Musheerabad | Sresta Bioproducts Ltd. | daily |
| – | other supermarkets, e.g. Food Bazaar | across the city | various | daily |
| **Commercial Organic Stores** | | | | |
| 15 | 24-Letter-Mantra | Banjara Hills | Sresta Bioproducts Ltd. | daily |
| 10 | Daram | Begumpet | Timbaktu Collective, Anantapur | daily |
| 14 | Fabindia | Banjara Hills | Fabindia | Tue-Sun |
| 19 | Fabindia | Himayathnagar | Fabindia | |
| 13 | Fabindia | GVK One mall, Banjara Hills | Fabindia | |
| **Direct Marketing and other** | | | | |
| 26 | 95 Park Lane | Kalasiguda, Secunderabad | own farm near Shamshabad | daily |
| – | Chetna Organic | home delivery to registered customers across the city | small farmers | once a month |
| 17 | HACA NPM vegetable outlet | Nampally | small farmers in Manchal Village, Ranga Reddy District | Mon-Fri |
| 8 | OREX Health Foods organic food counters | several IT Parks, Hitec City | various | daily |
| 9 | Organic Mobile | Balkampet | small farmers in Medak District | Tue |
| 1 | Organic Mobile | Gachibowli | small farmers in Medak District | Tue |

| No. in map | Name of store | Neighbourhood | Main suppliers of organic products | Opening days |
|---|---|---|---|---|
| 3 | Organic Mobile | Kukatpally | small farmers in Medak District | Tue |
| 4 | Organic Mobile | Malaysian Township, Kukatpally | small farmers in Medak District | Tue |
| 16 | Organic Mobile | Nampally | small farmers in Medak District | Wed |
| 18 | Organic Mobile | Rajendranagar | small farmers in Medak District | Tue |
| 23 | Organic Mobile | Ramanthapur | small farmers in Medak District | Wed |
| 25 | Organic Mobile | Tarnaka | small farmers in Medak District | Wed |
| 22 | Organic Mobile | Vidyanagar | small farmers in Medak District | Wed |
| 24 | Sahaja Aharam store | Tarnaka | small farmers in several districts in Andhra Pradesh | daily |
| 5 | Sristi Naturals stall | Kondapur | small farmers, various suppliers | Wed |
| 20 | Vijaya Enterprises | Chikkatpally | small farmers | daily |

*Source:* Own data

### 4.4.1 Commercial Organic Stores

To date there are no exclusively organic commercial shops in Hyderabad. This section portrays commercial stores where the major part of the food product range is organic. Supermarkets with a smaller organic product range, direct marketing outlets, non-profit cooperative initiatives and other organic retail formats are discussed in the ensuing sections.

Of all the retail outlets selling organic food in Hyderabad, the "24-Letter-Mantra Organic Food Superstore" in Banjara Hills has the broadest organic product range. The shop and the brand name "24-Letter-Mantra" are owned by Sresta Bioproducts Ltd., which started the first India-wide organic retail chain. The shop in Hyderabad opened in 2005. The product range consists mainly of a complete range of grains and pulses, but also comprises spices, tea, jams, bread, biscuits, snacks and ready-to-heat dishes. Part of the shop is a bistro selling small meals, snacks, biscuits, ice-cream and milkshakes, which are not all organic. In addition to their organic range, the shop also stocks conventional products in the categories fruits and vegetables, muesli, jams, and convenience food (biscuits, ready-to-serve dishes etc.). This is because customers want a complete range of food products, but the full product range is not (yet) available in organic quality. All products in the shop are advertised as "natural", but not all certified organic. They are organic whenever possible. Those that are certified organic correspond to the EU 2092/91, USA NOP and Indian NPOP standards. The products are currently priced 30–40 % higher than conventional products. According to the National Sales Manager, prices are likely to come down once the scope increases over the next five years. The long-term goal is a price premium of 10–15 % more than conventional. The 24-Letter-Mantra store offers home delivery twice a week, free of charge for minimum orders of 500 INR. Ten percent of customers make use of this service, which is more than the average in conventional supermarkets. Sresta Bioproducts are also looking into supplying to company canteens.

Part of the fruits and vegetables sold in the Hyderabad are grown on a company-owned farm of 7 acres in Medchal, Rangareddy District. Products from the vegetable farm are transported to the store in Hyderabad on a daily basis, by the regular public buses. Conventional fruits and vegetables are bought from the wholesale market in Hyderabad and sourced from a local supplier on the road to Medchal, which means that most of them are probably from the peri-urban areas around Hyderabad. For the other organic products, the supply chain is organised India-wide. Raw materials are sourced from all over the country and transported by road to the Sresta processing and packaging factory in Medchal. According to the National Sales Manager, processing is as decentralised as possible out of climate and energy concerns, the facilities are all over India, but packaging is centralised in Hyderabad for better control.

Sresta has thousands of contract farmers as well as their own field production projects across the country. Since the scope of the company requires a certain commitment in terms of scope and reliability, bigger farms or groups of farmers are more viable for them to source from. According to some NGO representatives, Sresta procures at low cost but sells at a very high premium. They also criticise the lack of community-involvement in contract farming. Farmers are dependent upon the prices the company offers as they have exclusive contracts with them. The profit for farmers and wages for farm workers in this supply chain is low.

Such criticism notwithstanding, the big merit of companies like Sresta is the sheer amount of land that they bring under organic cultivation: Sresta Bioproducts has more than 5,000 acres under organic cultivation across India. At this stage, Sresta makes more sales in export than in the domestic market, but domestic demand is growing continuously. In 2009, the monthly turnover of the 24-Letter-Mantra store in Banjara Hills was 800,000 INR. The number of supermarkets that Sresta Bioproducts supplies is also growing, and they are planning to expand into other supermarkets as well as to open two to three new franchising stores, one of them in Secunderabad.

Another store that can be called organic is Fabindia, although their range of food products is very limited. Fabindia was founded in 1960, primarily as an export house for handloom textiles. They expanded their presence all over India and internationally, and in 2004 started a small organic food product line. In Hyderabad, Fabindia has four outlets, two in Banjara Hills, one in Himayathnagar and one at the International Airport. Fabindia's objective is "to offer customers a complete organic lifestyle" (cited in Carroll 2005). All products are at least partly handmade, and an important component of the company profile is their support for poor artisans and rural livelihoods. The unique selling points of Fabindia are high product quality, a unique ethnic style and store decor and ambience. The style of their textiles is consciously timeless, so that garments can be worn for a long time. So far, Fabindia has a limited product range of organic food items: muesli, pasta, jams, fruit concentrate, spices, tea, and natural medicines. Efforts are being made to expand the range, as the organic food market sector is seen as one of the major opportunities for future development for Fabindia (Kalita et al. 2008: 6).

No data was available from the management about their supply chain, sales figures, number of customers reached or potential plans for expanding the product range. According to Kalita et al. (2008), Fabindia's sourcing strategy is heavily supplier-centric, and it follows a centralised hub model of supply chain management. This is apparently causing some problems with long delays in supply, so that the organic food products are not always available. The highly centralised supply chain means that quite a lot of energy is spent for transportation from producers to the stores, which are located in all major cities across the country. With regard to public relations, Fabindia relies mainly on word of mouth as a means of advertising. They do not have a customer acquisition strategy but focus mainly on customer retention. About 85 % of the customers are repeat customers (Kalita et al. 2008: 5). Fabindia use in-store posters and leaflets to raise awareness of the origin of the products, such as their rural suppliers or organic farming. Fabindia's strategy does not seem to be to offer a complete range of food items like 24-Letter-Mantra but rather a selection of high-value niche products such as pasta and muesli that appeal only to a small but affluent segment of the population. Only 8.3 % of customers interviewed by Kalita et al. (2008) mentioned wider product range as a possible area of improvement for Fabindia, which shows that they do not see the shop as the source of their regular nutritional needs.

Fabindia and 24-Letter-Mantra have a very similar customer profile comprising mainly highly educated, often Western-educated, modern, well-off and health- and lifestyle-conscious people, with an affinity to eco-friendly culture. Accordingly, both shops are located in upmarket locations that can best be reached by individual motorised transport. Price levels vary between products, but are generally significantly higher than conventional products. "Fabindia initially focussed on providing an Indian experience to the foreign buyer. In the 80s, it realised there is an untapped market among the upper and higher middle class. With the economic boom in the 90s, the focus has shifted to the upwardly mobile consumers in metros [...]. The target audience is college going youth and young professionals and just married couples in the higher middle class category." (Kalita et al. 2008: 2) According to the 24-Letter-Mantra store manager, their typical customer is highly educated, high socioeconomic profile, and mixed in terms of age. Their primary motivation for buying organic food is health concerns, which is underscored by the broad range of natural medicines and health supplements such as stevia, wheat grass powder, aloe vera or soy products. According to the store managers, certification is very important to the consumers in these shops, in contrast to most buyers in supermarkets.

### 4.4.2 Supermarket

Across the city, many supermarkets stock organic tea and some also herbal and ayurvedic medicines and cosmetics. A broader range of organic products is only available in selected stores. While some supermarkets dedicate an entire shelf to organic products, others may only have one or two varieties of staples such as rice or pulses. Several of the larger and more upmarket supermarkets have started selling organic food products over the past few years. The number of supermarkets stocking organic products has risen at a noticeable speed: While early in 2009 only the larger, upmarket supermarkets such as Spencer's, Q-Mart and SPAR had organic shelves, in 2010 even some smaller supermarkets had started selling a small range of organic staples. Spencer's Hypermarket in Musheerabad is listed separately in the Table 4 because of its wide organic product range compared to the smaller Spencer's supermarkets that are found across the city.

Q-Mart and Spencer's both decided to include organic products in their product range because customers asked for it. According to the managers of Q-Mart and Spencer's, their prime motivations are health concerns as well as a fashionable image of organic and health foods. Q-Mart tries to cater to this clientele through modern shop design and appealing, easily intelligible in-store information on organic food. The Regional Manager Merchandising for Andhra Pradesh of Spencer's thinks that organic food is "a fashion rather than a need, people don't buy it because of the inherent benefits of organic food but because of a lifestyle image." The supermarket managers interviewed confirmed that the clientele buying organic products is mixed, but dominated by middle-aged, educated members of the upper middle and upper class, often foreign-educated.

The supermarket managers all felt that the organic sector has been growing for a few years now, but the overall share of the total food market is still small. Spencer's only started selling organic products in 2007, and the SPAR hypermarket only opened in 2008. The total food sales of Spencer's are 60 million INR per month, of which organic makes up only 0.2 million INR, or 0.33 %. SPAR would like to expand its range in organic products, which as yet is very small, but they would only do so provided that supply is constant and reliable and at competitive price levels. Spencer's believes that organic food will be an important category in the future, but they do not have any immediate plans of expanding their range. They might once the sales increase. None of the supermarkets specifically advertise their range of organic products, except for some in-store posters in Q-Mart. The manager of SPAR said: "We would like to advertise it, but the problem is that an increasing demand should be supported by enough supply. There is no point in getting more customers to demand organic if we can't satisfy a bigger demand yet."

Most supermarkets have only one organic supplier, mostly large certified companies that operate on the national level. For example Q-Mart and Spencer's sell 24-Letter-Mantra products sourced directly from Sresta Bioproducts, Metro Cash and Carry sources from the Mumbai-based Ecofarms Pvt. Ltd. and SPAR from the Bangalore-based organic supplier Simple. The supermarket managers stated do not believe that certification is very important to most consumers, however for them it is vital because they need to be able to rely on claims made by the suppliers to avoid the risk of getting into legal problems.

The climate impact of supermarkets can be compared to upmarket commercial organic shops. The organic products they supply tend to be sourced from across India, which means that supply chains involve long transportation and temporary storage. Several stages of processing, packaging and storage also result in high energy-consumption, higher retail prices and less profits for the farmers. The sophisticated infrastructure of supermarkets results in a much higher energy consumption compared to traditional retail formats such as Kirana stores or street vendors. In its publicity, SPAR boasts that "The vegetables and fruits at SPAR are hand-picked at source and maintained at controlled temperatures till they reach the store. SPAR also uses state-of-the-art technology to keep the produce fresh even in-store. For example, the Fish counter at SPAR offers freshly cut and cleaned fish packaged in ice so that it stays fresh till it reaches your home. [...] Most of the produce is sourced directly from farmers / wholesalers, quickly placed in cold storage to retain the nutritive value of the food and brought to the store, all this within 18 hours from when the produce is picked up" (Reachout Hyderabad 2008). In addition to the actual energy consumption of the supply chain and retail store, the shopping habits of the average consumer such as the mode of transport they use to go shopping also has a significant impact on the overall environmental impact of food retailing. As will be analysed in more detail below, consumers buying in supermarkets tend to go shopping by car more than in other retail categories, and supermarkets are prepared for this by providing convenient parking facilities.

### 4.4.3 NGOs and Direct Marketing

Various NGOs work with small farmers in peri-urban and rural areas of Andhra Pradesh in order to promote sustainable agriculture. The approaches to rural development and marketing of organic products that NGOSs like CSA, DDS, Chetna Organic or SERP pursue are very similar. They work in different geographical regions and with different crops, but all have the primary mission of supporting smallholder producers, making their farming systems more sustainable and improving their livelihood and food security. Their programmes include technical support, promotion of locally adapted crops, and awareness raising to promote healthy and sustainable eating habits among the rural and urban population. Part of their strategy is to encourage farmers to form producer cooperatives in order to be able to pool their produce for joint marketing, access technical support or make larger investments for example in processing facilities. They are not have a commercial, business-oriented approach but focus on long-term sustainable rural development rather than short-term profits. Increasingly, considerations of marketing and business also play a role in their considerations. From their past experiences, many NGOs learned that it is not sufficient to support farmers in marketing efforts without focussing on consumers at the same time.

These organisations usually do not aim for certification with the India Organic label but instead work with Participatory Guarantee Systems (PGS) and independent laboratory sample tests for quality assurance. They reject the official India Organic certification system because it is too costly for the farmers. For the PGS certification, farmers only pay a fee of 1,000 INR (Misra 2009). PGS systems are based on participatory principles and community ownership is thus much higher. The famers they work with also do not necessarily adhere strictly to organic farming standards[21]. SERP regularly commission independent laboratory tests to guarantee that vegetables do not contain any pesticide residues.

For some time there was a farmer selling organic products at Erragadda Rythu Bazaar (Lohr and Dittrich 2007), but he had to stop meanwhile. At present, there are no farmers markets in Hyderabad where organic products are available. CSA work with farmers' cooperatives in a radius of up to 150 km around Hyderabad, primarily in Warangal district. Up until now, these farmers sell their produce in rural and local small town markets. CSA assisted farmer's cooperative in launching the brand Sahaja Aharam, Telugu for "natural food". With the support of CSA and the NGOs CROPS and SERP, a number of outlets have been set up in peri-urban areas. There used to be a stall outside CSA where farmers sold organic produce once a week (cf. Lohr and Dittrich 2007), but it was difficult for the farmers to come there regularly, therefore they decided to rather focus on developing local markets. Apart from supporting small farmers, CSA also does consumer awareness raising, for example through brochures about the Sahaja Aharam brand and organic agriculture.

In April 2009, they launched a consumer cooperative, the Sahaja Aharam Consumer Cooperative. It started with 300 members, but the target is 2,000. The cooperative is planning to open up a permanent organic food shop in the CSA office building, and to organise weekly home deliveries of vegetables directly to consumers' homes. This will be more convenient for the consumers, and also help the farmers in developing production and business plans.

The consumers' cooperative is planning to purchase a van for transporting the supplies and doing home deliveries. Once the outlet is established and running well, the target will be to open more subsidiaries across the twin cities, for example in Banjara Hills. The long-term goal is for the shop to have a broad range of products, with a focus on first- and second-level processed food. At this stage there are still very few third-level processed foods such as sauces or pickles, but the objective of CSA is to move farmers up the value chain and thus increase their net profits. The main target group in terms of customers are the lower and upper middle classes. According to CSA, this is a different group than the customers at shops like 24-Letter-Mantra who mostly belong to

---

[21] See Chapter 2.2 and 4.2.

the upper class. Due to the short supply chain and direct marketing as well as the less costly certification system, the price levels for organic products sold by these farmers will be significantly lower than in organic shops and supermarkets. Price levels at the Sahaja Aharam outlets are not much more expensive for many products, often only 1–2 INR; rice, for example, costs 26 as compared to 24 INR on the local market.

The regional rural development organisation Deccan Development Society (DDS) has been working with small farmers in Medak District since 1983. Their main mission is to promote sustainable farming methods and to revive the traditional regional food culture which is based on cereals, millets and pulses. Millets have been neglected by farmers for the past 25 years favour of rice and wheat. The market does not reward millet cultivation: price levels in 2009 were 27 INR for rice (producer price 8 INR) compared to 25 INR for millet. The cost of millet production on the other hand is lower because there are no inputs needed, but many farmers are not qualified to calculate their production costs very well are tempted by the higher market prices alone. Also, there is not much commercial demand for millet compared to rice, cotton or sugar cane.

Since rice was promoted and subsidised by the Public Distribution System for decades, consumer preferences have changed, and millets are not perceived as fashionable among urban consumers any more. DDS promotes the cultivation and consumption of millets because they are better adapted to the semi-arid climate of Western Andhra Pradesh, help improve the livelihoods of small farmers and are nutritionally superior. In order to create a market for the farmers they work with, DDS established a shop and organic café, Café Ethnic, in Zaheerabad four years back, and runs a mobile sale system called "Organic Mobile". The café attracts both health-conscious locals and interested passers-by with its range dishes based on local crops such as millets, wheat and pulses that are grown organically by small farmers. The Organic Mobile van stops in Sangareddy, Medak District, on Mondays and tours several neighbourhoods in Hyderabad on Tuesdays and Wednesdays.[22] It currently reaches about 50-100 consumers in Hyderabad regularly. Sales amount to 7-10,000 INR on average for three days of sales in Hyderabad and Sangareddy, Medak District. The main problem at this stage is product supply which is often irregular and not adequate to demand. Products are processed in Pastapur village in Medak District, about 150 km from Hyderabad, and transported in the Organic Mobile van.

---

[22] See map of organic outlets Figure 4.

In addition to supporting farmers and their marketing, DDS also works in awareness raising on nutritional quality of millets.[23] At events such as the Brinjal Biodiversity Festival they sell organic millets and pulses and provide information to consumers. They also published a brochure with information on different millet varieties, their nutritional properties and traditional recipes collected from farming women in Medak District with the aim of increasing awareness and consumption of millets and pulses.

Chetna Organic is an initiative with a somewhat more business-oriented approach. It consists of a foundation for farmer support, the Chetna Organic Farmers Association (COFA), as well as a farmer-owned company, the Chetna Organic Agriculture Producer Company (COAPCL). Chetna started as an organic cotton grower initiative with farmers in Andhra Pradesh, Maharashtra and Orissa. As their farmers produce various food products like pulses and spices, they started to focus on tapping the urban market for these, too. Their Marketing activities for food are limited to Hyderabad at this stage. Presently, Chetna supplies to around 700 households in Hyderabad in a home-delivery scheme. Customers are registered with Chetna and receive a mixed basket of products once a month. Chetna process and package the products themselves. To improve customer acceptance, they developed the NPM initiative Safe Harvest Pvt. Ltd. and the brand "Zero" which guarantees zero pesticide use through a PGS group certification process. Eighty percent of the produce are organic and the rest NPM under conversion to organic, but it is all sold as NPM. Chetna prefer to promote NPM in the Indian context rather than third-party certified organic because it is better suited for the small scale of production and can reach more people.

Another NPM initiative is the vegetable outlet at HACA Bhavan. It is a joint project of HACA and SERP: HACA provides the space in their building, and SERP is the link between HACA and the farmers. SERP is an NGO implementing the state-wide rural poverty reduction project "Indira Kranthi Patham" of the District Rural Development Agency (DRDA-IKP), a Government Agency for Rural Development. The project focuses on the poorest of the poor households and aims to enable them to improve their livelihoods through community organising. They also assist farmers in implementing NPM production in 3,000 villages across 18 districts, and there are 300 NPM shops run by farming women's self-help groups across the state (Misra 2009). Part of SERP's mission is to link producers in peri-urban areas to consumers (mostly middle-class) and encourage producers to access new marketing channels.

---

[23] See informational brochure on http://milletindia.org/EatSmart-EatMillets.pdf, and MINI et al. (2008).

The NPM vegetable outlet at HACA Bhavan is managed by farmers from Manchal village, 50 km from Hyderabad in Ranga Reddy District. Srinivas Reddy, the young farmer selling the vegetables on four days a week, collects produce from ten farmers there. The product range depends on supply and includes various vegetables such as carrots, brinjal, tomatoes, okra, chillies and green leafy vegetables. The vegetables are not certified, at this stage it is a trust-based system, but independent laboratory tests are used for verifying that no pesticides have been used in cultivation.

Initially the outlet was only open on one day a week, but in 2008 this was expanded to four times a week. It has since proved a big success; sometimes the vegetables are sold out within a couple of hours. The outlet is frequented by 100–125 customers per day, with a mixed customer profile from lower middle class to teachers, small businessmen, government officials and political leaders. HACA or SERP do not do any activities in consumer awareness raising, but Srinivas said: "It isn't our objective to sell in supermarkets, we prefer a separate outlet. The purpose is not only to sell, but to make people aware that our products are different."

A major incentive for consumers buying here is that the vegetables are always very fresh and taste better (cf. Misra 2009), that the location is convenient for many people living or working nearby, and also that they are hardly more expensive than conventional produce. This last point is due to an agreement with HACA stating that the prices may not be more than 2–3 INR more per kg than the prices fixed by the government for the Rythu Bazaars. Srinivas Reddy said he would in fact need another 2–3 INR extra in order to fully cover his production costs, though. Compared to certified organic products, there is not much more net profit in NPM production, which is why he is not producing at a larger scale at this stage. HACA wants to adhere to the price limit, at least until the outlet is firmly established. Partly this is due to fears that the number of customers might go down if prices were higher. However, the demand already increased since the outlet was started, and there are plans to expand sales volumes and product range in the future. At this stage, HACA or SERP do not promote the vegetable sales actively, because the supply is limited and they would not be able to satisfy an increase in demand.

From the point of view of building a sustainable urban food supply system with a low climate impact, the strategy pursued by these NGOs is sustainable in several ways. For one thing, small farms have been shown to be more efficient and more productive[24]

---

[24] Several large-scale comparative studies cited by Pollan (2006) as well as individual success stories (e.g. traditional farming systems in Medak District, cited by Adhavani (2009)) support this argument.

(DDS 2008: 3). Small-scale production also means more ownership for farmers, control of means of production and better labour conditions. Small organic farms tend to be more diversified and less mechanised, and they have a lower energy consumption than organic farms that operate on larger scales and depend on external organic inputs (biopesticides, biofertiliser). According to CSA, the government and bioinput companies push for this kind of agriculture to support the growth of the market for commercial bio-inputs. NGOs working in sustainable rural development rather recommend that farmers produce their own bio-pesticides and fertilisers such as manure and vermicompost from farm-internal raw materials.

Conventional supply chains are very long and thus involve a lot of waste of energy through transport and storage and monetary losses to middlemen. Usually products are supplied by a farmer in the peri-urban area to local collectors, then to the wholesale market in Hyderabad and finally to retailers or street vendors both in Hyderabad and peri-urban areas. If products are sourced from elsewhere in India, especially for supermarkets, the supply chain is more or less the same but might involve more middlemen and transport is often refrigerated.

In addition to its environmental benefits, small-scale farming and direct marketing with its decentralised supply chain strengthens rural communities, creates more employment and increases profit for farmers through higher producer prices. The products also reach broader strata of consumers because of the lower end consumer price levels. At the moment, around 30 % of the end price goes to the farmers, but that includes their production costs, so their net profit is only 5–10 %. When selling directly to consumers it can be as much as 80 %.

The support for small-scale sustainable agriculture has a broader importance for the entire region. The peri-urban fringe of Hyderabad where much of the urban food supply is produced has important functions as a green belt (ecological, micro-climate, recreation) and for the supply of the city with fresh food products, without the need for long transportation. Thus buying organic products from the region within a radius of 100-150 km contributes to the sustainable development of the entire urban and peri-urban area.

### 4.4.4 Other Formats

A small store in Gudimalkapur called Organic Talk used to sell some organic products like hand-pounded rice and pulses, but it closed down in 2009 because sales did not reach a profitable level. A new organic retailing business called Sristi Naturals recently started in Kondapur. Its marketing channel is a weekly organic stall selling vegetables, millets, rice, pulses, spices, honey etc. at KPHB colony in Kondapur. Products are sourced from various suppliers, for example fresh vegetables from the Sahaja Aharam producer cooperatives, millets from Timbaktu collective, and other packaged products from various organic companies. According to the owner, the business does not make any profits yet, but customers are showing keen interest.

Another newcomer in 2009 was OREX Health Foods, a young innovative organic start-up that has successfully started tapping a new niche market: In the IT parks in Hitec City, a large number of young professionals eat at least one meal per day in an office canteen. However, most of the food is rather heavy and does not tally well with health- and fitness-conscious lifestyles of many of the workers. OREX offers organic meals and snacks at counters in several IT parks in Hitec City. The servings contain a high share of fresh vegetables, millets and unpolished rice. They also cater to the demand for Westernised, modern food products, for example with light sandwiches rather than traditional Indian meals. A point they are still working on is the packaging. They use disposable plates and cutlery, because they have no facilities or man-power to wash reusable dishes. The owner is hoping to solve that logistical problem in the near future.

Both Orex and Sristi Naturals can be considered part of the organic movement of Hyderabad, in that they make an effort to cooperate as much as possible with small farmers directly, and are not primarily profit oriented. OREX seems to have found a very good compromise between supplying as much as organic as possible, but at the same time focusing on customer demand and thus ensuring economic success of the business model.

The small store Vijaya Enterprises in Musheerabad is an example of a shop catering to health-conscious consumers looking for high-quality health food and other health products. Beside food items like grains, pulses, peanuts, dates, honey and sweets, the product range comprises soy-based food supplements, wheat grass powder, sprout-makers, yoga-mats and the like. Products that are sometimes available in organic quality are: brown rice (hand-pounded), wheat, millets (Finger, Foxtail, Little), pulses (green gram, black gram, red gram, bengal gram), jaggery, and sometimes vegetables and leafy vegetables. The supply chain of Vijaya Enterprises depends on the type of products. The rice, for example, is sourced from small organic farmers from villages around Zaheerabad. Transport is done by truck, by a local transport company. Two new stores with a very similar product range, supplier and marketing strategy opened shop right next to Vijaya Enterprises in 2009.

The philosophy behind the shop is not just commercial interest but mainly providing healthy food at reasonable prices, and spreading awareness of healthy food and "helping the people", as the owner and manager said in a personal interview. The organic products at Vijaya Enterprises cost about 20 % more than conventional, but according to the owner only about 10 % of the customers buy organic products there and they do not mind the higher prices. According to the shop owner, even the conventional products he sells are grown by small farmers using very little chemical inputs, and they are not more expensive than elsewhere. The customers have a mixed socio-economic background. However, only about 10 % of them are aware that some of the products are organic, according to the owner nobody really enquires after that. Some of the customers come from quite far, as far as Hitec City or even outside Hyderabad, to go shopping there, and the shop appears to be very busy every day.

# 5 Consumption Patterns and Consumer Attitudes

## 5.1 Changing Dietary Patterns and Purchasing Habits

### 5.1.1 Food Preferences

Changes in lifestyle have resulted in an on-going process of nutrition transition among India's new urban middle classes (see for example Lohr and Dittrich 2007). Dietary preferences are changing and a number of new dietary habits have emerged. Some of these changes have contradictory effects if assessed from a sustainability point of view. Middle class diets are generally becoming more diverse, and an increasing consumption of fruits and vegetables (J. Singh 2004) is beneficial for consumer health and for the diet footprint. Protein-rich foods like meat, dairy products and fish account for an increasing share of food consumption (J. Singh 2004), resulting in a potentially higher climate impact. Over the past decades, millets have been largely replaced as a traditional staple food items by an increasing consumption of polished rice, and more recently wheat products. The replacement of traditional crops was spurred by the influence of urbanisation as well as market factors. The Public Distribution System contributed to the replacement of millets by rice, because it supplies very cheap rice to low-income citizens.

One of the trends associated with globalisation and greater affluence of the middle classes is the increasing popularity of packaged and convenience food such as ready-to-eat dishes. Convenience foods, or "tertiary processed foods" (Paradkar et al. 2007: 39), are food products that require minimum preparation, typically just mixing or heating. "With the advent of industrialisation and the absolute influence of the West in the form of processed and fast foods, the traditional Indian diet is slowly but steadily losing its importance" (Harish 2003: 50). Between 1995 and 2005, spending on eating out in Hyderabad doubled (Kalanidhi 2006). A new preference for "western products like hamburgers, pizza, French fries etc." (Pai 2007: 29) is also visible in the increasing numbers of fast food restaurants, food snack bars, coffee shops and ice-cream parlours particularly in well-off neighbourhoods like Banjara Hills or Himayathnagar. Lohr and Dittrich (2007) found in their survey among supermarket customers in Hyderabad that the majority still eat mostly home-cooked Indian food[25] on a daily basis and eat out only once or twice a month. However, most retailers in their survey reported a trend towards increasing purchasing of instant food, ready-to-eat food, snacks and sweets over the past five years. They also noticed a trend towards more packed products in general, for example for grains and spices. Forty-eight percent of the respondents in the survey conducted by Sudershan et al. (2008) in Hyderabad purchase packaged food. Polasa et al. (2006) found that in Southern India as many as 71 % of respondents buy packaged food, in the study conducted by Lohr and Dittrich (2007) 75 % of middle-class families purchased processed and convenience food. According to Vijayapushpam et al. (2003), 28 % of children in higher-income households eat such instant food products every day.

Even though fresh food is usually cheaper, convenience and packaged food have become popular for two main reasons: Firstly, rapid urbanisation, changes in working hours and increasing numbers of working women mean that consumers are willing to spend less and less time on food preparation (Paradkar et al. 2007; Pai 2007). Secondly, socio-cultural dietary preferences have changed and packaged products are associated with higher prestige, a perception that is spurred by advertising images. Food companies get into packaged convenience food products because of their higher value addition and supply chain factors like longer shelf life without loss of flavour or reduced wastage from spoilage. From the point of view of consumers, processed and packaged food is not only perceived as more convenient but also as more hygienic, modern and fashionable. While fresh and home-made food is still considered superior in quality by many, there is "a perception among many women that foodstuffs sold loose and in unpacked condition are usually adulterated" (Sudershan et al. 2008: 512).

---

[25] For an analysis of food habits among lower middle class households in Hyderabad, see (Hofmann and Dittrich (2009; 2010).

Highly processed foods are often rich in sugar and fat and low in fibre. In combination with a physically inactive lifestyle, they can contribute to nutrition-related health problems or lifestyle diseases such as obesity, diabetes and cardiovascular diseases. Of all Indian cities, Hyderabad has the highest rate of patients with diabetes as well as an alarming number of overweight children and obese people (Raghunatha Rao et al. 2004). Another problem is "secondary malnutrition", the phenomenon of malnourishment despite sufficient or even excessive calorie intake. This trend could be "one of the biggest problems that India's middle-class will face in the years to come" (Griffith and Bentley 2001: 2694).

Processing and packaging also increases the environmental footprint of food products. On the other hand, processed foods can have positive effects from a gender perspective: As women are mostly responsible for food preparation, processed foods can significantly reduce their work load. Of course, whether this should be interpreted as a truly emancipatory effect remains doubtful, as it does not challenge existing household power relations and household-internal allocation of tasks and responsibilities.

As a result of the limited product range, the products bought most commonly in organic quality are unprocessed or low-level processed foods, mainly millets, rice, other grains, pulses and vegetables. Fresh organic fruits are not available except sometimes at 24-Letter-Mantra. The range of products that respondents reported to buy is probably distorted slightly by the selection of interview locations. Interviews at the 24-Letter-Mantra store[26] would probably have resulted in a broader range of products including vegetables and more processed products. Most respondents buy organic products only in the place where they were interviewed, and a few also at 24-Letter-Mantra.

### 5.1.2 Shopping Habits

Together with dietary preferences, shopping habits are also changing. One of the most visible aspects of changes in consumption patterns is the expansion of supermarkets and hypermarkets in the city. As Lohr and Dittrich (2007) illustrate, several phases of development of the retail scene in Hyderabad can be distinguished over the past few decades. In the first phase, small neighbourhood stores dominated the retail market. The second phase began around 2001 with the opening of the first large malls in Abids and Musheerabad. These malls are essentially structured like department stores, usually with a food supermarket in the basement. The current third phase of the "retail revolution" (Lohr and Dittrich 2007) only began in 2005/06. It is marked by a rapid increase

---

[26] Permission to conduct interviews with consumers there could not be obtained, cf. Chapter 3.

in the number of supermarkets – over 100 new ones in Hyderabad over the last few years (Srivastava 2009) – and an increase in the average size of supermarkets with a trend towards hypermarkets and larger malls. For example, SPAR, the world's largest independent food retail chain, opened up Hyderabad's largest hypermarket to date of 20,000 square feet in Begumpet only in October 2008 (Reachout Hyderabad 2008). The opening of new hyper-malls in the well-off neighbourhoods, such as GVK One in Banjara Hills or Inorbit Mall in Hitec City, in the past two years is an indication of an increasing affluence and lifestyle-orientation of young middle-class consumers. It also expresses their preference for shopping in modern, secure, clean and air-conditioned surroundings. Shopping in malls and eating out in fast food outlets or fancy restaurants are increasingly perceived as a leisure activity rather than a necessity. Supermarkets these days promise "to elevate shopping from a daily chore to a world class shopping experience that also offers value for money." (Reachout Hyderabad 2008)

For grocery shopping, the younger generation below thirty years of age mostly prefers supermarkets to Kirana stores (Lohr and Dittrich 2007). They are mostly well-off and prefer to buy in bulk on a weekly basis. Lohr and Dittrich (2007) found that the products most commonly bought in supermarkets are processed and convenience foods as well as non-food items. The most important reasons for shopping in supermarkets are time pressure/ convenience, fashionable image, special offers, credit card facilities, the air-conditioned, hygienic atmosphere, arrangement of goods and higher variety.

Despite this trend, the vast majority of the population still does not frequent supermarkets on a regular basis but relies mainly on traditional retail formats such Kirana stores, markets and street vendors for their daily needs. As was to be expected based on their above-average socio-economic status, the majority of 78 % of respondents does part of their regular grocery shopping in supermarkets, most of them at least once a week. Nevertheless, almost all of them buy fresh fruits and vegetables at markets, which many frequent at least once a week. One respondent at Mehdipatnam Rythu Bazaar said, "Since I have time now, I prefer to buy vegetables of my own choice. I used to buy them in supermarkets, but they are not as nice, they look more hybrid. I feel the vegetables here are more natural because they look very different, not so standardised." Fewer respondents regularly buy from the traditional retail formats Kirana stores (50 %) or street vendors (27 %). Lohr and Dittrich (2007) found that between 75 % and 100 % of consumers in different income classes purchase fruits and vegetables at Rythu Bazaars or from street vendors. These markets were established by the Government of India in order to lower costs for consumers as well as increase revenue for farmers by eliminating middlemen from retailing of agricultural produce.

Reasons for preferring traditional retail formats such as Kirana stores, street vendors and markets vary. The main advantages of Kirana stores are proximity to home, high product quality, flexibility and long opening hours, long-term personal relationships with clients and, related to this point, the opportunity to buy on credit. The lower-class women interviewed in this survey said they do not purchase in supermarkets because it is too costly. They buy vegetables from small local Kirana stores and street vendors, and they also buy through the Public Distribution System. Although supermarkets may be cheaper for some products, especially when buying in larger quantities, the small volumes sold at Kirana stores are more convenient for consumers with cash flow problems. Supermarkets also do not have a uniformly good image: Many consumers who may never even have been to a supermarket before do not think that supermarkets supply fresh products, especially fruits and vegetables, and that they are more expensive than traditional retail formats.

The preference for supermarkets is connected with the dramatic increase in individual motorised traffic over the past five to ten years. Increasing numbers of consumers go shopping by two-wheeler or car. This has resulted in a greater fluctuation of customers at Kirana stores, because there are fewer pedestrians and it can be very difficult for potential customers to find a parking space. Lower-income groups that are less likely to own a vehicle and whose radius of action is therefore smaller usually go shopping on foot near their homes. Consumers with a vehicle are more likely to do their shopping in bulk on a weekly or monthly basis, which favours supermarkets and hypermarkets where all daily consumption needs can be satisfied at once (one-stop-shopping). Conversely, this means that the trend towards supermarket shopping results in higher energy consumption and emissions of food purchasing due to transport.

Among respondents of this study, the most commonly used means of transport for getting to supermarkets is the car, followed by two-wheeler. A few respondents also take autorickshaws, walk or go by bus. Most respondents visit markets by car or two-wheeler as well. Most consumers buying at Kirana stores do so on foot, near their home or workplace. The percentages for consumers at 24-Letter-Mantra and Fabindia can be assumed to be similar to that for supermarkets. A bigger share of respondents interviewed at the HACA NPM vegetable outlet and the Organic Mobile live in the neighbourhood and walk there, although some do come from further off by car or two-wheeler. Almost two-thirds of respondents prefer to buy all their needs in one shop,

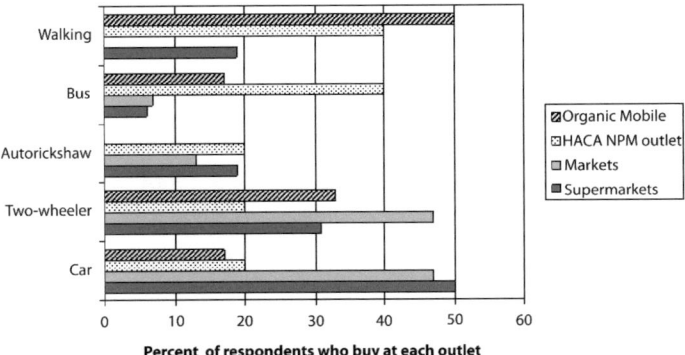

**Figure 5:** Means of transport used by purchasers of organic food for shopping in different locations
*Source:* Own data

which means they are likely to travel further. Only 38 % find it important to be able to do their shopping within walking distance from home or work.

### 5.1.3 Increasing Health Consciousness

Partly as a result of adverse health effects of dietary changes and increasingly inactive lifestyles, a contrary trend towards a new health consciousness is emerging (Lohr and Dittrich 2007; cf. The Nielsen Company 2007). It finds its expression in a new preference for natural and unprocessed food such as fresh fruits and vegetables, organic products, brown rice, millets, pulses, whole-grain bread, low-fat and low-sugar products. All respondents without exception gave health as their only or at least primary motivation for purchasing organic food. Almost two thirds gave health as the sole motivation. Another 24 % mentioned environmental consciousness and 12 % taste in addition to health. The quantitative survey revealed that those that buy organic food belong without exception in the group that is also concerned about chemicals, which is another indication that the prime motivation is health concerns.

Many consumers buying organic food for health reasons actually had problems with nutrition-related diseases before, and thus became sensitised for adverse effects of recent dietary trends. Several respondents mentioned diabetes as a motivation for changing their dietary patterns and buying more wholesome food products like millets, unpolished rice and organic products. Lohr and Dittrich (2007) also found that most consumers that buy organic food do so because they already suffer from health problems. Consumers often learn about organic food from naturopaths during treatment of food-related health problems.

Of those respondents that buy organic food regularly or occasionally, almost all think that organic food is better for them because it does not contain any harmful chemical residues (no adverse health effects). None of the respondents mentioned superior nutritional quality in terms of micronutrient content as a reason why they think organic food is better for their health (positive health effects). Across different socio-economic sections of the population, there are widespread concerns over food quality and contamination risks. The majority of respondents in the quantitative survey expressed a concern over potential residues of harmful chemicals in their food. The values varied between interview locations and social background of respondents (see Figure 6). Respondents at Vijaya Enterprises who are a particularly health-conscious group had the highest value of 100 %. Among the lower-class respondents, only 50 % were worried about chemicals. Overall, concern increased with social status and education level. In the slum area where interviews were conducted, the women interviewed were aware that they should wash fruits and vegetables because there are chemicals on them. More than half of the respondents said they were worried about chemical residues in their food. They heard from elders that food used to be grown without chemicals, but none of them had heard of organic food.

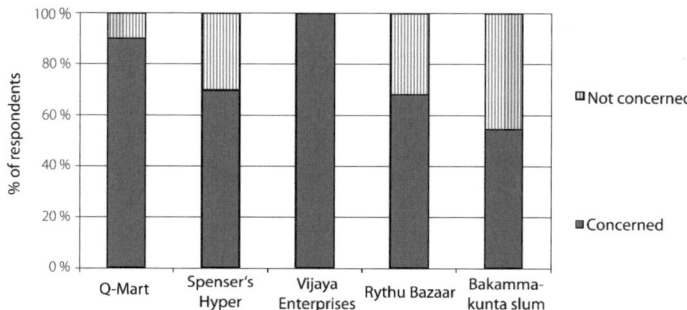

**Figure 6:** Concern over chemical residues in food in the quantitative survey
*Source:* Own data

Hofmann and Dittrich (2010) demonstrate in their case study on food-related risk perception among lower middle class women that this group has a high awareness of risks related to pesticide and chemical contamination of food. Also, healthfulness, nutrient-content and freshness play an important role. In how far the preference for fresh food over convenience is determined by the inability to afford much processed and packaged food is not entirely clear. However, several of Hofmann and Dittrich's respondents consciously choose higher costs and more effort in preparation over convenience. Members of the lower middle class who cannot afford to buy fruits on a daily basis also make an effort to ensure a minimum vitamin supply by regular purchasing fruit juices.

Many lower middle class families may have migrated to the city only in the past one or two generations, and hence still have strong ties to their rural home region. Their families are also more likely to be actively involved in agricultural production. Hofmann and Dittrich (2010) show that comparisons between food in the village of origin and in the new urban setting are very frequently made by lower middle class women, and mostly to the disadvantage of the range available in the city. There may be much greater diversity, but the product quality in terms of freshness, naturalness, taste and safety (chemical contamination, adulteration) is perceived as inferior.

While most upper middle and upper class families have some ties to rural areas as well, their links to agricultural production may be more distant. Their families often have been residing in the city for much longer, and have lost that close link to agricultural production and hence also the expectations of food being fresh and natural. For them, mass media and advertising influences may play a much stronger role in shaping their food preferences. This point would have to be further investigated in a study comparing consumer attitudes and preferences across a wider social spectrum than was possible in the context of this study.

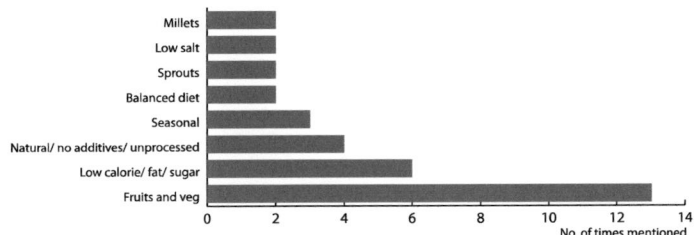

**Figure 7:** Concepts about "healthy food", asked in an open question
*Source:* Own data

Factors that respondents considered to constitute a healthy diet (in addition to organic/ chemical-free) are shown in Figure 7. One respondent summarised a definition of a healthy diet as follows: "Low nonessential fat, low sugar, low carbohydrate, high protein, fresh, essential oils." For about three fourths of respondents, calorie-content is an important consideration when shopping for food, among both purchasers and non-purchasers of organic food. Overall, organic consumers tend to rely more on natural means of eating healthy rather than food supplements. Only 43 % of them buy functional food/ food supplements, as compared to 75% among non-buyers of organic products. Fresh fruits and vegetables are similarly popular in both groups.

The trend towards healthy lifestyles in general is also evident in the increasing popularity of health clubs, fitness clubs and gyms. The trend towards convenience food means that there is also a significant potential for food supplements and functional food products. A study by AC Nielsen (The Nielsen Company 2006) found that Indians are among the world's top ten buyers of health supplements. Health conscious consumers look for food products low in calories, fat, sugar and sodium, as well as high in fibre, vitamins and minerals, but "even the nutrition conscious consumers will not want to give up their taste preferences and convenience" (Pai 2007: 31; cf. K.V. Singh 2009). The sales figures of functional food demonstrate a growing popularity of health food discourses. However, taking them as an indicator for an increasing actual health concern of the population is problematic: More than anything, the overwhelming success of functional foods in the Indian consumer market indicates a lack of nutrition information among the population, as many of the health claims of these functional food products and food supplements are hardly more than clever marketing tricks (Rajiv 2009). For example, many consumers consider the fast food outlet Subway healthy, merely because the otherwise high-calorie, low-nutrient sandwiches contain some greenery and come in vegetarian varieties. Hofmann and Dittrich (2010) also found widespread misconceptions among lower middle class women; for example, Maggi noodles are considered healthy by many because they are vitamin-fortified, and the malted hot drink Horlicks, which has sugar as its main ingredient, is perceived as healthy because it is manufactured by a pharmaceutical company.

There are similarly wide-spread misconceptions about what "organic" means[27], about "healthy food" and about agricultural production in general. Some people think that conventional agriculture in India or AP does not use a lot of chemicals so that they do not see a need for organic farming. Others take the opposite view and believe that the land, air and water are so polluted by DDT and other chemicals that it is not possible to farm truly organically at all. The latter view appears to be particularly wide-spread in lower social strata (Hofmann and Dittrich 2009).

A good deal of confusion appears to exist among consumers about the differences between such terms as "organic food", "natural food" or "health food" (Chakrabarti and Baisya 2007). "Natural" means that a product has undergone minimal processing and does not contain any additives or preservatives, but the term is not protected in

---

[27] Cf. Chapter 5.2.

any way and there is not certification. "Health food" usually refers to products with low sugar, high fibre, high vitamin and mineral content. Many diabetic products and functional food fall in this category. Products that are fresh and generally considered healthy – especially fruits and vegetables – are often mistaken for organic as well. In interviews and informal discussions many consumers claimed to have seen or even be buying organic in places that do not in fact sell any organic products. For example, some consumers thought that the fruit and vegetable shops Pure and Natural or Choupal Fresh stock organic products. Even the shop assistants, whether in shops that sell or do not sell organic products, are not always aware of what organic means. At Fabindia, for example, a shop advertising to provide "a complete organic lifestyle", one shop assistant was unable to give information on whether the textiles are made of organic cotton. Instead he stressed that the cotton is "pure" and "natural". Two customers interviewed at a health shop thought that all products there are organic even though very few really are.

Sudershan et al. (2008) found that more than half of the consumers they interviewed never check the ingredients of packaged food. Similarly, in the survey by Polasa et al. (2006) 23% of respondents in the Southern region always check the list of ingredients, 25% sometimes, and 52% rarely or never. These figures suggest a rather low level of awareness and serious concern over food intake. Many consumers appear to rely more on the perceived image of a product as good for them than on actual nutrition information. This lack of consumer education and the widespread health myths raise doubts as to whether claims of increasing health-consciousness could partly be the product of discourses on healthy food in the media and in advertising. Articles in magazines and newspapers such as Indian Food Industry, Food and Beverage News or The Hindu claim that there is growing health consciousness among consumers, but many of these articles (especially in Indian Food Industry) are written by representatives of the food industry. This raises doubts whether they are merely pushing a discourse constructing a newly health conscious category of consumers who are eager on health supplements, nutraceuticals and innovative functional food that are highly processed, expensive and hence highly profitable for the food industry (cf. Pai 2007; Tewari 2007).

The food industry capitalises on the lack of nutrition education and the widespread myths and misconceptions about wholesome food in order to boost sales of functional foods and food supplements. The use of non-committal expressions such as "natural", thus invoking an association with the general semantic field of healthy and organic without guaranteeing any real quality standards, has become a highly popular marketing strategy. Many supermarkets place organic food in or near the health food category. Q-Mart places its organic product range in the section with health and diabetic products. 24-Letter-Mantra also has health supplements and products for diabetics. The most clearly health-oriented shop concept of all stores selling organic products is Vijaya Enterprises, a shop that is more oriented towards a wholesome diet and healthy lifestyle rather than strictly organic products. In fact the store does not always stock organic products, but only when there are supplies available. However, the owner and manager Mr. Bubarao has personal relations with the producers of most of his products and says that they generally do not use a lot of chemicals so that the products are superior to conventional even though they are not strictly organic. The DDS Organic Mobile also targets a health conscious clientele, for example people eating millets rather than rice as a diabetic-friendly option. Many aspects of traditional Indian food culture that are not just healthy but also sustainable in other respects, for example vegetarianism, use of pulses and the traditional staple millet etc., have no lobby and are not perceived as fashionable.

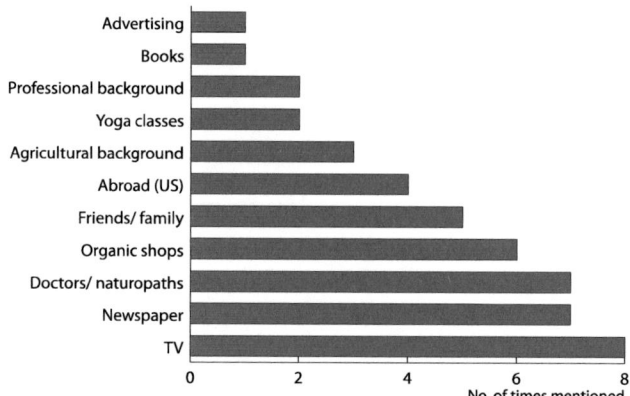

**Figure 8:** Sources of knowledge about organic food (several replies per person possible)
*Source:* Own data

An analysis of marketing strategies and media discourses can yield valuable insights on how demand for health products is created. Especially television and advertising have a major influence on urban consumers' consumption patterns. The most important sources of information about organic food mentioned by respondents were television and newspapers as well as doctors or naturopaths (see Figure 8). The people interviewed by Sudershan et al. (2008) learned about food labels from the following sources: 53 % from TV, 16 % from health workers and 21 % from friends and relatives. In the survey conducted by Polasa et al. (2006), respondents in the Southern region also got information on food labels mainly from TV (73 %), radio (7 %), friends and relatives (13 %) and newspapers (3 %), but only 2 % from health workers. This is a good indication as to which channels of communication could be effective for spreading awareness and information about sustainable food consumption.

The media can be an important source of knowledge about food and nutrition, but they can also have a strongly manipulative role in boosting the social prestige of certain types or food and spreading misinformation. According to the assessment of DDS, most people believe television advertising on processed food products such as milk-based fortified drinks for children, which are considered prestigious and "rich" food.

### 5.1.4 Emerging Environmental Consciousness

As has been demonstrated in the previous section, buyers of organic food are mostly motivated by concerns over health much more than by concern over the environment. An indication of the presence of a general environmental consciousness could be the fact whether people find it important to buy regional products that have not been transported too far. The fact that more than half of the consumers of organic food do not prefer regional products supports the assumption that the majority of organic consumers are not motivated by a general environmental consciousness. For the remaining ones that find regional origin important, it is not always clear whether they prefer regional products for environmental reasons, to support the regional economy, out of mistrust of quality of imported products, out of local patriotism or other reasons.

These findings correspond closely to the results of other research. The survey conducted by Chakrabarti and Baisya (2007) in the National Capital Region found that the prime motivation for purchasers of organic food in India is health and nutrition, and that an environmental awareness has yet to emerge. Jain and Kaur (2004) found that environmental awareness and knowledge are far lower in India than in developed countries. A study in Mumbai found that the major motivation for purchasers of organic food in Mumbai is health: "Environmental reasons or concerns for the well being of farmers were not stated and are likely to be of minor relevance to Indian consumers in general" (Garibay and Jyoti 2003: 17).

In February 2010, an article in The Hindu discussed the contribution of food to climate change: "Load your plate with veggies. It could be a simple way to save the planet from global warming, according to some experts." (Hema 2010) In general, climate change and how it intersects with food and nutrition is not a dominant discourse in India yet.

Although some people may be aware of the interlinkages between food consumption and climate change, the contribution of individual behaviour on the climate is not prevalent in people's everyday perception.

Mawdsley (2004) demonstrates in her review of literature on environmental issues in India that the middle classes have so far been neglected in research on environmental awareness and activism. As they constitute a major target group for organic food marketing and promoting sustainable food consumption more generally, this is an important field for further investigation. The broad and heterogeneous socio-economic category of the middle classes has to be broken down into more differentiated groups because "a very wide variety of values, beliefs and behaviours can be found amongst India's middle classes, reflecting regional, linguistic, gendered, ideological and other pluralities" (Mawdsley 2004: 97). This plurality means that while there is no dominant environmental public discourse yet, specific segments within the middle classes may well be very interested in this issue and open for changing their consumption patterns out of environmental concerns.

## 5.2 Awareness of Organic Food and Purchasing Constraints

Awareness of organic food was found to be quite high among respondents of the quantitative survey. As many as 57% had heard of organic food and had at least a basic understanding of what it means. Rao et al. (2006) found even higher figures for some cities in India. However, these figures are not representative of the general population, as a comparison across interview locations reveals (see Figure 9). Lohr and Dittrich (2007) found in their survey of supermarket customers in Hyderabad that 76% had never heard of organic food before, and only 3% ever purchased organic food. Those that had heard about organic food all belonged in the higher middle class stratum. Some of the supermarket managers interviewed said that it does happen that customers do enquire after availability of organic products, but they are a very small minority.

The level of awareness was higher in places that sell organic food, and where customers belong to higher-income and higher-education groups. The figures for Mehdipatnam Rythu Bazaar and the slum area are probably a better indication of the average level of awareness among the overall population. The people that are most likely to be aware of organic food are those that are young, educated, know English (read and write, too) and had some international exposure, for example living abroad or visiting relatives. The survey conducted by Garibay and Jyoti (2003) among consumers in Mumbai found that 25% were aware of organic food. They belonged to the highest socio-economic groups.

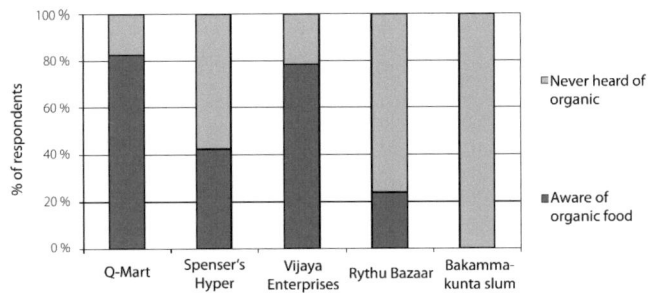

**Figure 9:** Awareness of organic food in the quantitative survey
*Source:* Own data

Even among farmers, there is a great lack of awareness of organic farming. Some farmers interviewed at Mehdipatnam Rythu Bazaar said they did not use any pesticides, or very few for some crops such as potatoes. At the same time, they did not believe it to be possible to grow certain other crops without pesticides, and they said they had never heard of organic farming.

Reasons for not buying organic food, or buying it rarely, are varied: Some young people who do know about organic food hardly do any grocery shopping because they still live with their parents. The number one reason for consumers not buying organic products is their lack of awareness of organic food. Even though increasing numbers of Indians are concerned about their health, especially in relation to food and nutrition, very few are aware that an alternative to conventional food exists.

Among those that *are* aware of organic food and willing to buy it, the biggest obstacle to really buying (more) organic is the lack of availability. As the map of organic food outlets (Figure 4) reveals, there are very few and rather scattered outlets for organic food in a city of over 7 million inhabitants, where traffic and public transport are a hassle and where the nearest Kirana store is often no more than a few meters away from people's doorstep. One respondent said, "It requires a separate trip to the only organic store there is. If the supermarket starts keeping organic food, I will buy." Several of those who buy organic regularly or occasionally mentioned that they would like to buy more organic products if they were more easily available: "I tried to find organic food in three or four places. I would buy everything organic if it was available!" Most consumers that are aware of organic food know very few, if any, places for purchasing these products. By far the most well-known shop is 24-Letter-Mantra, although people often have difficulties remembering the store's name. They variously refer to it by "the store in road number 12", "the store in Banjara Hills", or variations on the name such as

"24" or "24 Mantra". There is also a lack of information on where to buy organic food. At the Brinjal Biodiversity Festival, for example, several visitors expressed an interest to buy organic products more often but were not aware where to find them.

Convenience of purchasing proved an important factor for customers buying at Sristi Natural store. The colony where the stall is set up can be classified as upper class. Customers so far show great interest in the products, and above all emphasised the high product quality and the convenient location of the stall within walking distance of their home. As many of them are young professionals in the IT sector, the stall timings can probably be improved to better suit their requirements in terms of time. One of the customers said: "Most of us are working, so weekends would be much better than Wednesday. We only get home at 9 or 10 in the evening."

One respondent said he does not know how to tell if a product is organic. In light of the complexity of defining sustainable agriculture systems in India[28], it is easy to imagine that consumers get confused about how to recognise organic products, especially since most are not aware of organic certification at all[29]. Garibay and Jyoti (2003) found that the main reason stopping consumers from purchasing organic food in Mumbai is also lack of awareness.

The Nielsen Company found in its 2005 Global Consumer Opinion Survey that together with a lack of availability of organic food, the price premium is one of the main obstacles for consumers choosing organic options in India (The Nielsen Company 2007; Chakrabarti and Baisya 2007). Garibay and Jyoti (2003: 17) found that in department stores in Mumbai organic products cost up to twice as much as conventional. As discussed in Chapter 4, the price levels of organic food in Hyderabad differ significantly between the different retail formats and across product categories. Of those respondents that buy organic regularly or occasionally, 72 % think it is more expensive, compared to only two thirds among those that do not purchase organic products. One woman buying millets from DDS said "Here it's hardly more expensive, but the supermarkets add on. 24-Letter-Mantra is too expensive." And it is not only the product prices however, that are a consideration for consumers: "I don't mind spending a little extra, but it also depends on the distance to the nearest organic outlet; if I have to add transportation costs it becomes very expensive."

On the other hand, for many health-conscious consumers higher prices are not a major constraint: "Compared to the health benefits organic products are not expensive."

---

[28] See Chapter 2.2.
[29] See Chapter 5.3.

According to a newspaper report on organic vegetable sales, "customers do not mind paying for healthy vegetables" (The Hindu 2009). Most respondents that are aware of organic food in fact said that price is not a primary criterion. Only one fourth of those who do not buy organic said that the prices were too expensive. A few respondents said that they would not mind paying more, or that the price does not matter to them as long as they get good product: "I don't mind spending more on organic." For almost half of those that purchase organic products regularly or occasionally, price is not an important consideration, and for another one fourth only a secondary consideration, provided that product quality is high. Price is an important consideration for half of those that do not purchase organic products, and not a very important consideration for the other half. When compared across the different income groups, it turns out that the price level is more of a concern for the lower income groups. Most of those for whom it is not important at all belonged in the upper middle class category[30]. This indicates that this socio-economic section is affluent enough to be able to prioritise quality and healthfulness over price. They are an important target group for marketing efforts for organic food (cf. Rao et al. 2006).

Both Spencer's Hyper and SPAR tried to sell organic fruits and vegetables, but they did not go well because the prices were almost double and consistent supply was difficult. In this market sector, the higher prices are particularly relevant for consumers because vegetables are a daily commodity. Carroll (2005) cites similar experiences made by shops in the fruits and vegetable market sector. One should keep in mind that the vast majority of Indians belongs to lower social classes and might indeed not be able to afford even 2 or 3 Rupees more per kilogram. As one respondent said: "The prices are justified, but to reach many people it would have to be cheaper." Nevertheless, the purchasing power of that minority that can afford a high premium makes them an important target group for the upmarket organic sector.

The obstacles to organic food consumption show prove Thaler and Sunstein's hypothesis that better knowledge does not necessarily result in better consumer choices[31] to be valid for the vast majority of consumers in Hyderabad. Although a small number of highly dedicated consumers are willing to make considerable efforts in order to purchase organic products, the majority of consumers are not prepared to compromise too much on convenience or price levels. In addition, individual food preferences and

---

[30] See classification in Table 2.
[31] See Chapter 2.5.

long-established habits such as eating polished rice prove very hard to change, because they are perceived as part of the food culture.

## 5.3 Importance of Labels for Purchasing Decisions

A major precondition for consumers buying organic food, especially if they have to pay a higher price for it, is credibility and transparency of standards of production. There are two main strategies how customers can verify whether the products they purchase were really produced according to organic standards. One is a trust-based personal relationship to the producers. This is the strategy that many small farmers rely on in direct marketing. The other strategy is an official certification process, where the different stages of the supply chain from production to packaging as well as the final product are inspected by independent third-party agencies. In contrast to the export markets, where certification is a vital precondition, uncertified organic products do have quite some success on the domestic market (Carroll 2005).

Organic certification is not an important criterion for the majority of consumers because most are not aware of organic labelling. In the quantitative survey, only 10 % had seen the India Organic label before, and 8 % the PGS label. Among those that purchase organic products regularly or occasionally, knowledge was slightly better (see Figure 10 and 11). Values varied significantly between interview locations, although no data on knowledge of the PGS label was collected for Q-Mart and Spencer's Hyper. Again the number of those that were aware of either or both of the labels were highest in the higher-income and more educated groups, in line with the values for awareness and purchasing of organic food discussed above.

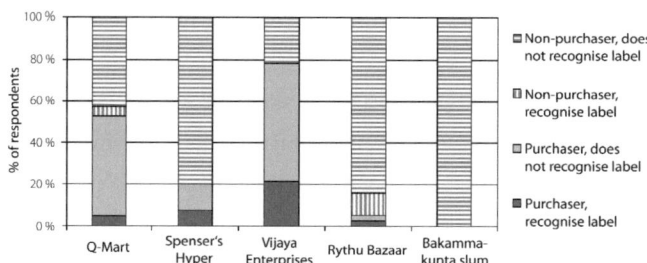

**Figure 10:** Awareness of India Organic label among purchasers and non-purchasers of organic food in the quantitative survey
*Source:* Own data

Even among those respondents of the semi-structured interviews that buy organic products regularly or occasionally, only two (at HACA and Organic Mobile) recognised

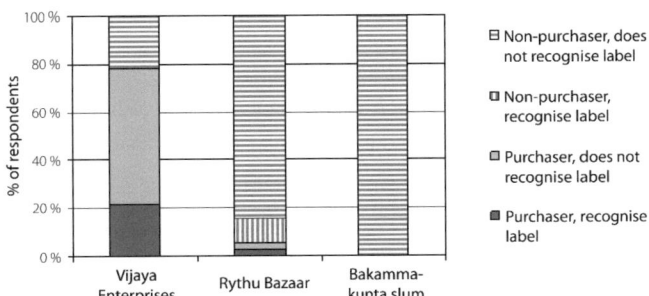

**Figure 11:** Awareness of PGS Organic label among purchasers and non-purchasers of organic food in the quantitative survey
*Source:* Own data

the India Organic label. However, neither was aware of what it signifies. Seven respondents recognised the PGS label, almost all of them customers at the Organic Mobile or Brinjal Biodiversity Festival. This is not surprising, as the DDS products bear the PGS label. However, 5 of the 7 did not actually know what the label means. The only two respondents who knew what the PGS label means are regular DDS customers.

Sudershan et al. (2008: 511) found that only 20% of respondents buying packaged food recognise the symbols on food labels. Similarly, Polasa et al. (2006) found that country-wide 21 % of their respondents know food labels. In the Southern region, most of these are aware of ISI mark[32] (97 %), followed by Agmark[33] for agricultural products (39%) and FPO[34] (Fruit Products Order) license (13 %). In a personal interview, Sudershan and Rao from NIN said that the more educated people are, the greater the likelihood that they recognise labels. The most commonly known label is the ISI mark, whereas Agmark and FPO license are hardly known by consumers. In contrast to consumers in industrialised countries, Indian consumers tend to trust more in the producers, because supply chains are shorter, many people come from farming backgrounds, and more processing is done at home. There is still great trust in producers and vendors, even if consumers do not know them personally. According to Sudershan and Rao's judgement, brands are also an important trust factor for many consumers. Even though consumers may be aware of the labels, illiteracy and lack of knowledge of English may prevent them from actually checking the information on food labels, most of which are in English (Polasa et al. 2006).

---

[32] Indian Standards Institute by the Bureau of Indian Standards(www.bis.org.in)
[33] For agricultural products that meet certain quality standards (see http://agmarknet.nic.in).
[34] Fruit Products Order, for processed fruit products (www.fssai.gov.in/Fruit-Prod.aspx).

Another important question with regard to labelling is whether consumers trust in the reliability of the certification process, and whether they recognise labels. Less than half of all respondents place an importance on product brand when doing their shopping, whereas over 80 % finds it important to be able to trust the producers or vendors. Three fourths of all respondents said they trusted organic labels, or would trust them after they were given a brief explanation of their meaning. Seventeen percent said they would probably trust the labels once they got more information about how certification works. Overall, a great deal of consumer education and awareness raising is needed for organic labelling to fulfil its function of assuring consumers that the products are worth the price premium. This is in line with the findings of Sudershan et al. (2008: 512) who emphasise "the need to spread awareness about checking quality symbols and information on food labels."

## 5.4 Target Groups for Sustainable Food Consumption

An analysis of the socio-economic background of consumers reveals that both awareness of organic food and actual organic purchasing are concentrated in higher socio-economic groups. Thirty percent of respondents in the quantitative survey purchase organic products regularly or occasionally. These values are highest for interview locations where organic food is sold, and where the average socio-economic and educational level of customers are high. Most respondents in the semi-structured interviews that buy organic food belonged to the lower (24 %) and upper middle class (40 %) category[35]. The three income categories above the upper middle class were represented by 8 % each, and only 4 % belonged in the lowest household income category. This indicates that the income level of organic food purchasers is much higher than the average Indian income distribution (see NCAER 2005). Rao et al. (2006) also focus on the highest socio-economic groups in their analysis of the domestic market potential of organic food.

However, this does neither mean that *all* members of the upper class have a potential for being won over for sustainable consumption, nor that *all* organic consumers belong to the high-income and highly educated group. "Surprisingly, it is not only the upper society which is increasingly health aware and ready to pay a higher price for quality food. Middle-class families seem to be the more promising clientele, as experience from a number of smaller initiatives selling organic products in towns and cities have shown" (Eyhorn 2005: 75).

---

[35] See Figure 1.

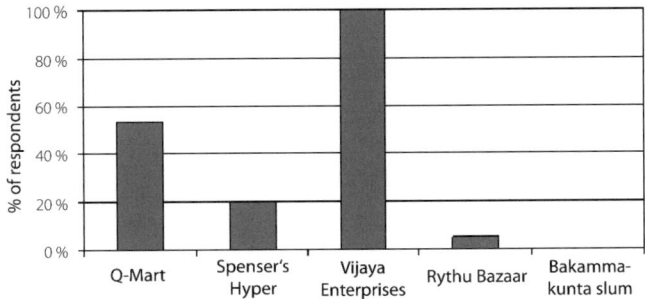

**Figure 12:** Consumption of organic food compared across interview locations in the quantitative survey
*Source:* Own data

The distribution of respondents with regard to level of education was similar to the income groups, and overall relatively high. The majority had a graduate degree (40%), or even postgraduate or doctorate (40%), and only 20% had a high-school diploma or quit after tenth grade. In line with their educational level, most respondents spoke English at an excellent level (24%), or at least well enough to be able to do the interview in English (44%), and less than one third (32%) needed a translation into Telugu or Hindi. Twelve percent had lived abroad for more than one year.

The intake of high-quality food increases with income and education, and the educational level of the heads of household has a particularly positive influence on food consumption patterns in the case of women, but not in the case of men (Mujeeb-Ur-Rahman and Visweswara Rao 2001). In many households, women do most of the cooking and have more responsibility for household food purchasing. According to information by CSA, they also tend to show more interest in organic food. Typical characteristics of consumers purchasing organic food globally according to Bhattacharyya (2004: 158) are: health-conscious, educated, affluent, taste-conscious and with a strong concern for the environment.

Based on the above analysis of consumer awareness, consumption habits and concerns motivating purchasing decisions, this section presents a tentative outline of consumer segments that can be identified as the most promising target groups for promoting sustainable food consumption patterns in general and marketing organic food in particular. While their overall consumption patterns can mostly not be considered sustainable in a strict sense, certain aspects are already more sustainable than among the average population. In particular, their previous knowledge and affinity for organic food mean that they have comparatively high potential for activating them for sustainable consumption in the future. The classification into target groups is based on criteria in the following fields: Food consumption behaviour (purchasing of organic food, vegetarianism), food- and sustainability-related attitudes and values (health-consciousness, environmental-consciousness, food preferences), socio-economic and socio-demographic variables (education, profession, income, experience abroad, age, family status). Based on these factors, five tentative groups were identified. They are portrayed and illustrated in exemplary case stories of consumers (see Boxes) below.

The groups were derived on the basis of qualitative consumer interviews in Hyderabad, anecdotal evidence and data from participatory observation. The data material was not sufficient for statistical analyses that would allow for a clustering of consumers into actual food lifestyle segments[36]. The classification should be further extended, refined and substantiated by more empirical evidence. Nevertheless, despite the small data set specific groupings could be seen to emerge from the qualitative interviews.

### I. Committed vegetarian organic food purchasers

Activists and volunteers such as AID India or resident welfare associations as well as or members of the Sahaja Aharam Consumer Cooperative are often highly dedicated to an environment-friendly lifestyle, including food consumption. Their socio-economic background is upper middle class to upper class, they are highly educated, often with advanced university degrees and an excellent command of English. Many have strong international influences in their biography, either through having lived abroad themselves for extended periods or through family members that live abroad. They do not belong to a specific age group, but range from young families to middle aged and active pensioners. Their socio-cultural background is generally high caste, often Brahmins who have specific conceptions of purity that are very dominant in the field of food and nutrition. Mostly, these people are vegetarians, either out of socio-cultural tradition and religious reasons, or health reasons, or both. Among some of them, there is a tendency to romanticise the agrarian roots of their family, even though they may have lived in the city for generations and lost the close ties to agricultural production themselves.

In Mumbai and Bangalore, strong vegan networks have developed[37]. To my knowledge, no such groups exist in Hyderabad to date. It would be interesting to find out if such a segment of consumers exists in Hyderabad and whether they fit in the committed vegetarian target group or form a group of themselves.

---

[36] See Chapter 2.5 for analytical approaches to lifestyle segmentation in the field of sustainable consumption.

[37] See www.mumbaivegans.blogspot.com and http://veganbengaluru.wordpress.com.

**Box 1: Committed vegetarian organic food purchasers I**

Deepti[38] recently became a member of the Sahaja Aharam Organic Consumer Co-operative. Deepti is principally responsible for the food purchasing and cooking in her small family of three. She normally buys most of her groceries in a nearby supermarket because it is more convenient to buy everything in one place. Deepti is a vegetarian, and generally cares a lot about what she and her family eat and where the food comes from. She has not yet visited any of the producer co-operatives that supply to the Sahaja Aharam store, but she would like to go soon because for her it is very important to know where the food comes from. One day she came across a weekly vegetable sale from a Rythu Bazaar truck in her street, and she was very pleased that she could ask the vendor where the food actually came from. Normally when she buys in regular shops she misses having that opportunity. Linking her food purchasing back to producers is one of the main advantages she sees in being a member of Sahaja Aharam.

**Box 2: Committed vegetarian organic food purchasers II**

Anand and Sangita are a young couple who live with their 2-year-old child and Anand's mother. They employ maids to help in the household and with the child. Their family background can be considered upper middle class and well-educated. After they got married, Anand and Sangita lived in the US for a few years while Anand did his Master's degree in engineering. Anand's mother holds a PhD in sociology, and Sangita's parents have university degrees as well, but both their parents are also active organic farmers. In the US they bought mostly organic food. Now that they are back in Hyderabad they would very much like to keep up the habit, but are having difficulties in Hyderabad because there are very few shops that sell organic products, especially vegetables. For them, organic food is not just about protecting their own and their child's health:'it's not just about buying that particular food product, it's about encouraging a certain way of cultivating food (...) it's very much interconnected with the environment." Their commitment has led them to become active members of the Sahaja Aharam Consumer Cooperative. Generally they don't buy from supermarkets, they prefer neighbourhood grocery stores, partly because they don't want to support supermarkets, and because they don't like the system there of putting everything in plastic bags. They to try to bring their own bags when they go shopping. "Why do we need to put everything in plastic?" They don't normally eat out in restaurants much, and they don't buy fast food. Anand's mother says "We used to cook lots of snacks at home, but now we don't take the time for that anymore." However, when they buy snacks outside they buy them where they are freshly made, not processed and packaged snacks.

---

[38] All names in the consumer case studies have been changed to fictional names.

## II. Young civil society activists

In Hyderabad, there is a relatively strong environmental activist scene of NGOs such as Greenpeace. Their approximately 1,000 volunteers share a strong concern for environmental issues. They come from different socio-economic backgrounds, generally middle class, and have different educational levels. While some of them may be very dedicated and have strong convictions when it comes to food, and might actually belong more in the first target groups, others have not given the area of food too much thought yet. For many, one potential point of initiation to this topic may have been the public debates around the agrarian crisis and farmer suicides, or around the introduction of Bt Brinjal to India. Most of those that do not have a strong awareness for sustainable food consumption yet are convenience oriented; they are open to buying organic food and within certain limits even to pay a premium for it, but they are not committed enough to make any particular efforts in order to buy organic food if it is not readily available.

### Box 3: Young civil society activists

> Naveen is a young computer engineer who works for a microchip manufacturer in Hitec City. On weekdays when he is at work he eats lunch at restaurants. When he meets friends for lunch or dinner, they sometimes go to fastfood places like McDonald's or Pizza Hut, although Naveen stresses that he does not eat burgers. At home, he likes to cook his own food. He lives by himself in Dilshuknagar, and buys food in Kirana stores and on the market. For vegetables he likes to go to the Rythu Bazaar and to the fruit wholesale market near his house. Naveen is interested in the idea of organic farming, although he admits to not knowing very much about it. His interest is mainly out of concern for the environment. Naveen is a member of Greenpeace, and he tries to mind the environment of his lifestyle in his everyday life. For example, he does not own a car or motorbike and travels only by public transport. Naveen would like to buy organic food, and would not mind paying more for it. However, he would not go out of his way for it, the stores should be at a convenient distance from his home. For example, the Sahaja Aharam store is 5–6 km from his house, which he would consider too far.

## III. Health-oriented converts

Many of the customers at outlets like DDS Organic Mobile or the health shop Vijaya Enterprises fit into a category that is characterised by a distinct personal history of converting to a health-oriented lifestyle. Often they are naturopathy patients[39] who already

---

[39] Several customers at Vijaya Enterprises and the Organic Mobile mentioned the famous TV naturopath Dr. Manthena Satyanarayana Raju, naturopat/ Naturecure Specialist, see www.teluguone.com/health/manthena/index.jsp.

had health problems such as diabetes and started changing their diet and overall lifestyle on their doctor's or a naturopath's advice. They are interested in yoga and are vegetarians for health reasons. They are more into natural and health food such as sprouts, whole grains, millet and fresh fruit juices than organic food as such. Their motivation for buying organic food is mainly that it is perceived as more natural. Consumers in this category sometimes lack more detailed information about why certain products are supposed to be good for them, and are susceptible for nutrition myths and dubious health claims made about products like wheatgrass, soy extracts or aloe vera. Some organic companies exploit this susceptibility in their marketing strategies. In socio-economic terms, this group belongs in the middle class, but not necessarily upper middle class. Also their education level is often lower than for example in the first group of the committed organic purchasers. In interviews this became evident as translation from Telugu or Hindi was necessary more often than for the first group.

### Box 4: Health-oriented converts

> Kishore is in his fifties and works as a real-estate agent. He started buying organic food one year ago. A few years back he was diagnosed with diabetes. He started using Homeopathy, and changed his whole lifestyle after that. He learned about healthy eating habits from TV and naturopathy lectures at Osmania University. He is now on a low-oil and low salt-diet, and eats a lot of organic products, sprouts, fresh juices and the like. He does not buy a lot of organic food because it is not readily available, but whenever he can find it he buys it. He is a regular customer at DDS Organic Mobile. He likes the fact that the DDS staff can give him information about the products they sell, and they also have leaflets with nutritional information. Price is not really an issue for Kishore, he finds that most organic products are more or less the same price as conventional ones.

### IV. Convenience-oriented young professionals

With its dynamic IT sector, Hyderabad is an attractive city for young, educated and well-trained professionals. Socio-economically, they can be classified as upper middle class. Many have international exposure for example through studying and living abroad or at least through friends who lived abroad for some time. Several respondents in this group became familiar with organic food in the US, where a broad organic product range is available at highly competitive price levels. These young professionals are often health-conscious and very fitness-oriented. They have memberships in gyms and health clubs, and like low-calorie and functional food. In their free time, they lead modern, globalised lifestyles and go out to pubs, music bars and restaurants. They may be vegetarians, but many are not very strict about traditional rules like vegetarianism, drinking and smoking. For this target group, organic food is an attractive option because it fits in with their fitness-oriented lifestyle. They also like the idea of doing something for the environment and contributing to climate change mitigation – provided that it does not come at the expense of convenience. They may also support charities or environmental NGOs, and express their social and environmental concerns in groups and social media such as the Facebook group "Better Hyderabad Initiative". However, their commitment is often unstable, and their everyday lives are characterised by consumerist, resource-intensive lifestyle habits such as driving a car, using air-conditioning, buying latest electronic devices, flying on holiday and the like. They are used to negotiating multiple contradictions between tradition and modernity in their everyday lives.

### Box 5: Convenience-oriented young professionals

> Sreedevi works in call centre at i-Labs IT park in Hitec City. She normally eats lunch in the canteen everyday, but is not very happy about the food there. She recently learned about the OREX[40] organic food counter on the top floor of his office building, and has started eating there regularly, as she likes the food very much. She says the meals are very nourishing, but do not fill her up too much so she can go back to work afterwards with fresh energy. Sreedevi is a vegetarian, and very conscious of her weight and health. Although she says with an apologetic grin that she does many things that are probably not very good for her health, she tries to make a difference wherever it's possible without too much effort. The environment and climate protection are not much of a concern in her everyday life; she says that to date she has not given it much thought, although she had read something about the climate impact of lifestyles in the newspaper. She does not know any details about organic farming, for her the main point is that the food at OREX is lighter, fresher and more wholesome than the regular canteen food. She has heard that organic food is grown without chemicals that could be potentially harmful. She would not mind paying a little extra for a wholesome lunch, but she adds that it should not be too much, so she is very happy that her company subsidises the organic food counter as part of the company health awareness programme.

### V. Occasional organic purchasers

Many of the people who buy organic food occasionally, for example at 24-Letter-Mantra or in supermarkets, like the idea of organic food but are not prepared to go to any

---

[40] See Chapter 4.4.

particular efforts in order to purchase organic food. They have a vague perception of organic food as better for them, but are not particularly concerned about eating conventional food. For them, organic food has to be available at a convenient distance and at affordable prices. Their socio-economic background and educational level is mixed. Overall, this group is the least specific and should probably be further subdivided on the basis of more detailed empirical evidence.

**Box 6: Occasional organic purchasers**

> Rahul is very aware of his eating behaviour. He is not a vegetarian, but he says he only eats meat about twice a week, mainly chicken and goat meat. He has a strong passion for sustainable agriculture, and together with a friend he has even started investigating options for starting their own organic farm. His main concern with regard to food is eating wholesome food without the risk of being exposed to potentially harmful chemicals. However, his preference for organic food seems to have much to with a comprehensive understanding of it as being more natural and pure, he connects it strongly with notions of natural cycles and balance, and producing as well as consuming in moderation.

The tentative segmentation into target groups outlined in this section can provide a starting point for making consumer awareness raising campaigns more specific, and for identifying key areas within the field of food consumption where it will be particularly effective to start with strategies for sustainable consumption. For example, if specific groups already have a strong affinity to vegetarianism and place strong emphasis on notions of purity of food due to religious traditions, these could provide starting points for organic food promotional strategies.

# 6 Conclusion and Recommendations

## 6.1 Promoting Sustainable Food Consumption

The food system of Hyderabad is currently undergoing profound changes related to economic growth and the globalisation of nearly all aspects of life. A greater diversity of food than ever is available to consumers, and the number of those who are in a socio-economic position to afford the new products is increasing rapidly together with the size of the middle classes. According to NCAER (2005: 2), "[t]he rapid rise in incomes will lead to an even faster increase in demand for consumer durables and expendables."

This trend poses new challenges but also new opportunities for promoting sustainable consumption patterns.

Many aspects of the Indian food sector and food culture are favourable for introducing the notion of sustainable consumption. For example, agricultural production is mostly small in scale, there is a strong tradition of low-input farming, many people are vegetarians and concerns over healthful eating are increasing across the socio-economic spectrum. To date, only a small segment of the population is willing to profoundly change their food lifestyle and compromise on factors like convenience. A trend towards sustainable consumption patterns as a fashion or towards an overall "green" lifestyle has not emerged on a significant scale yet. Solidaridad recently conducted a study on the potential demand for fair-trade tea and coffee among India's middle classes. The survey of 500 "fairly educated and well to do"[41] middle class members showed that about one third are concerned with labour practices, fair prices and sustainable agriculture practices in tea and coffee production. Fair-trade clothing is also available in the Indian domestic market, from brands like Industree Crafts or Fabindia, and organic cotton textiles in selected boutiques. Despite these first indications of consumer concern, at this stage these products are produced primarily for export and reach only a small fraction of the Indian upper middle and upper class. A trend towards a bigger market segment that might be compared with the phenomenon of the market for LOHAS (Lifestyle of Health and Sustainability) in the USA and some European countries might well emerge in the future.

For the Indian organic food sector to grow, organic products need greater visibility in the urban retail scene and consumers need information on how to distinguish organic from conventional or various "natural" and "health" products. There is also a lack of awareness of the environmental and social benefits of organically grown, regional and seasonal food. While the emerging trend towards healthy eating is certainly good news for the organic business, it should probably not be overrated. Increasing segments of society are concerned about their health, but awareness of the specific health benefits of organic food is often fragmented and insufficient, and based on image and appearance rather than knowledge.

An emerging trend towards healthy eating habits and sustainable consumption in general could be supported by media campaigns counteracting the positive image of convenience food and fast food. As a communication channel for disseminating information on food and nutrition, most respondents by far prefer TV, followed by newspapers,

---

[41] See www.isealalliance.org/news/survey-shows-indians-ready-to-sip-an-ethical-cuppa.

doctors and family members or friends. Lohr and Dittrich (2007) recommend that education on food and nutrition should become part of the school curricula. Studies on the impact of nutrition education in Hyderabad came to different conclusions for different socio-economic groups. While Vijayapushpam et al. (2003) detected an encouraging improvement in the knowledge levels of upper and higher middle class schoolchildren, the survey by Raghunatha Rao et al. (2004) showed a very low impact of nutrition education programs on adolescent girls of low income and lower middle-class families. Women and children are considered to be the most effective multipliers with regard to health and nutrition education (Mujeeb-Ur-Rahman and Visweswara Rao 2001). DDS has made good experiences with its Biodiversity Festivals, which are part of an awareness raising and educational campaign in rural areas, as well as with the FNCC (Food and Nutrition Counselling Centre) initiative for nutrition education among schoolchildren in Zaheerabad. Both initiatives try to fill the gap left by the school curricula. Consumer clubs, which are as yet rare in India, could also play an important role in spreading awareness of organic food and more healthy dietary habits.

While changing individual household consumption patterns can certainly contribute to making the food system of Hyderabad more sustainable, the power of consumers to change markets should not be overrated (Brand 2008; Geden 2009). Geden argues that the opportunities for consumers to counteract climate change are very limited, because the impact of their action is negligible compared to other factors such as industrial emissions or the market influence of large corporations. Furthermore, consumers' willingness to change their behaviour depends to a significant degree on external circumstances, so that even if their awareness is sufficient they may not necessarily act on it (Bogun 2008). In order to achieve sustainable modes of production and consumption and a low carbon economy, changes have to be made both in the private realm of individual consumption as well as on the political level. Therefore people need to take on responsibility not only or primarily as consumers who can change their lifestyles and shopping habits, but rather as citizens who can get involved on the political level and influence the shaping of regulations on food production, processing and retailing. Comprehensive strategies for sustainable consumption thus need to address not only individual consumption patterns but also structures that facilitate sustainable consumption. Much of our consumption behaviour does not have any immediate and clearly visible harmful consequences, which makes it easy to forget about these consequences entirely. Consumers therefore need incentives beyond long-term sustainability benefits for changing their purchasing decisions.

In India, one option could be to use the Public Distribution System as an instrument for promoting organic food and local, aggro-climatically adapted crops such as millets.

Together with individual consumer behaviour, the purchasing decisions of bulk buyers in the public and private sector also have a significant influence on the food market. Important stakeholders in this respect are the hospitality industry (hotels, resorts, restaurants), company canteens, school canteens and government authorities. In developed countries, the power of public procurement for boosting sustainable consumption and production has been recognised for some time. Germany recently passed legislation implementing the EU directive on public procurement which states that tenders *may* contain specifications regarding social and environmental standards of production. In India, a similar development is not yet discernible, but could be a long-term perspective for contributing to sustainable food systems. As yet, there is no government policy or directive on either sustainable procurement or procurement of food in general. It lies solely in the responsibility of the administration and canteen management of each organisation. An enquiry at the Centre for Cellular and Molecular Biology (CCMB), which has a large canteen with a very good reputation, revealed that they do not use any organic products because they are too expensive. Their customers ask for quality food, but at low prices. DDS also had discussions with district officials in Medak about procurement of organic products by the district, but the payment they could offer was not feasible for the farmers. An important field of enquiry for future studies is therefore the purchasing power, procurement mechanisms and regulations and the priorities of those in charge of food procurement in public sector organisations.

With regard to private-sector bulk buyers, Lohr and Dittrich (2007) report that some schools gave permission to multinational corporations for selling snacks, sweets and soft drinks in their canteens. In light of increasing numbers of overweight and obese children in Hyderabad, the interest among school administrations, parents and children for reversing this trend towards healthier and more sustainable options should be investigated. This is particularly relevant for the large private schools that have canteens providing meals for students, and where parents are most likely to be willing to pay more for high-quality meals. However, care should be taken that public schools and lower-income groups are not left out. One of the farmers working with the NGO SERP supplies vegetables to the midday meal scheme of a government school in Adilabad District. In order for more farmers to become engaged in similar initiatives, better networking between NGOs, farmers and the organisers of midday meal schemes is needed.

In light of the overall trends towards eating out more often on the one hand and towards increasing health-consciousness on the other, restaurants are another potential stakeholder for promoting organic food consumption. Organic restaurants along the model of Café Ethnic in Zaheerabad could have a major potential in the upmarket neighbourhoods. The fast food chain 6-Pack which marketed their products as low-calorie and healthy had already closed down again in 2009. This could be an indication that either the marketing concept was not accepted very well, or that products did not meet the expectations of customers in terms of quality or price level.

Among upmarket hotels and resorts, awareness of organic food is quite high. The chefs at the ITC Kakatiya, Novotel, Taj Deccan and Greenpark Hotel restaurants all know about organic food, but do not regularly use it. ITC Kakatiya have used some organic products before, and Novotel sometimes use 24-Letter-Mantra products but is not sure that they will continue to get supplies in the future. ITC Kakatiya stopped buying organic supplies because they were too costly and because consistent supply in required quantities proved difficult. However, they are willing to use organic products in the future provided that there is a reliable supply at acceptable rates. Greenpark Hotel and Taj Deccan would also consider it if there is enough supply and costs are "reasonable". They all said they never get any enquiries by guests asking for organic food. The director of Lahari Resorts outside Hyderabad runs an organic farming project on the resort premises. He did not try purchasing organic food for the resort yet, but said he would not mind paying more for organic food. He said the main problem at this stage was consistent supply of high quality. Organic certification is a crucial factor for hospitality industry stakeholders, as the management has to be able to provide a reliable guarantee of product quality to customers.

The current state of demand from bulk buyers again indicates that the main obstacle for organic market growth is constant and sufficient supply at acceptable rates. This is a huge opportunity not only for commercial organic companies but also for small farmers that can produce at low costs once the conversion period has been mastered and supply chain problems overcome. Small organic producers do not have the scope for supplying to bulk buyers, but through forming cooperatives they could achieve a more consistent supply, greater product variety as well as greater volumes of supply. In addition, networks between producers and bulk buyers need to be established or strengthened so that procurers from the relevant institutions will get in touch with suppliers of organic food rather than sticking with their customary suppliers.

## 6.2 Organic Sector Growth: On the Path to Sustainability?

Changes in urban consumption patterns, the purchasing habits of the newly emerging middle classes and the priorities of bulk buyers will have a strong influence on the scope and quality of future growth of the organic market sector. The organic segment in the domestic food market is growing steadily, and some analysts even speak of "a real boom" Eyhorn (2005: 74). The main drivers of this growth are rising incomes of certain segments of the population as well as a trend towards health-consciousness. While it would be exaggerated to speak of a "real boom" of the organic market in Hyderabad at this stage, organic food supply is definitely improving. Since the overview study conducted by Lohr and Dittrich (2007), all of the large hypermarkets and many supermarkets introduced a small but expanding range of organic products. Many interview respondents said they always buy certain products in organic quality, especially millets and rice, and some would even like to buy all their food organic if it was readily available. The products most frequently demanded in organic quality by Indian consumers are vegetables and fruits, followed by spices, rice, pulses and tea (Garibay and Jyoti 2003; Rao et al. 2006). Half of the respondents started buying organic products less than one year ago, and several experts expect the share of the population that buys organic food to grow to about four percent over the next ten years.

Chapter 4 demonstrated that the organic food sector in Hyderabad comprises a variety of different types of marketing channels, with two distinct models at either end of a continuum. At the one end is the corporate retail model run by commercial, profit-oriented organic companies and supermarkets. At the other end are NGO-driven farmer initiatives that traditionally concentrate more on agricultural production and rural development than on marketing in urban areas. Whether the growth of the organic sector will lead to a higher level of sustainability of the urban food system will depend on which one of these models will come to dominate the organic segment in the future. This, in turn, will depend largely on the institutional context as well as consumer behaviour.

The corporate retail model of organic food distribution has the potential to reach wide target groups, but its overall environmental performance is dubious. In countries like Germany or the US where the biggest part of the growth of the organic food market sector over the past years took place in supermarkets[42], part of the organic agriculture sector has moved a long way from the original principles of organic farming.[43] In the US in particular, much of organic agriculture is highly mechanized and energy-intensive and

---

[42] Cf. Holdinghausen (2009).
[43] Cf. the definition of organic agriculture by IFOAM in Chapter 2.2.

operates on industrial scales comparable to conventional agriculture (Pollan 2006). The energy consumption along the value chain – from production, processing, distribution and marketing all the way to transportation to the end consumer's home – means that these modern retail formats are not much more sustainable than other shops selling conventionally produced food products. The benefits for rural and peri-urban areas of production also remain limited due to country-wide supply chains and the specific structures of contracting systems.

The expansion of the middle classes in Hyderabad is closely linked to changes in purchasing habits such as a preference for one-stop-shopping, increasing levels of motorisation and expansion of malls and supermarkets. All of these contribute to a steeply rising ecological footprint for food shopping. While there is a strong trend among the younger generation for purchasing in malls and hypermarkets, increasing urbanisation and growing middle classes will also result in growing demand for small retail stores. Despite the expansion of supermarkets and hypermarkets in the city and the preference of young, well-to-do consumers for these modern retail formats, Kirana stores continue to play an important role for the daily food provision of Hyderabad. Accordingly, the Kirana owners interviewed by Lohr and Dittrich (2007) did not feel threatened by competition from supermarkets yet. They thought that customers value their cheaper prices, flexibility and proximity to customers. The increasing entry of supermarket chains into the retail market did stir up fears of competition in the future, though. Although the number of Kirana stores is still far bigger than supermarkets, their share of the total value of retail spending on food was estimated by Gupta (2005) to be already less than 50 %. However, malls and supermarkets are suffering more from the economic recession because a larger part of their product range consists of non-essential consumer goods rather than staple foods and convenience goods. Despite expansion plans of some supermarket chains, urban population growth rates are still bigger than the growth of their market share. Several supermarkets especially in malls had to close down again. In 2008/2009, over thirty supermarkets shut down in Hyderabad (Srivastava 2009). The space in the basement of the new GVK One mall reserved for a supermarket also remains unoccupied as yet. The "retail revolution" of the past few years (Lohr and Dittrich 2007) is slowing down somewhat, due to a combination of peaking rents and decreasing sales. Customers opt for cheaper varieties of products, and cut down on spending for luxury products such as health drinks (Srivastava 2009). The long-term impact of this crisis will remain to be seen, and will depend on the overall economic climate, in particular the purchasing power of the middle classes and the rents for commercial space.

Within the organic segment, modern retail formats target those consumers who are looking for organic convenience food and health products and who do not mind spending more money on products of higher quality, whether perceived or real. The increasing health and lifestyle orientation of some segments of the urban middle classes are likely to lead to an expansion of commercial organic companies, upmarket organic shops and organic sections in supermarkets. At this stage, an expansion of the organic product range in organic shops like 24-Letter-Mantra can be achieved mainly in the market sector of processed and highly processed convenience products, since the range of unprocessed or low-level processed staples such as grains, pulses, spices and tea is already fully covered. The demand for convenience food is also growing within the organic market sector. 24-Letter-Mantra introduced a range of microwavable ready-to-heat dishes in 2009, the first stock of which sold out within weeks. Their range of snacks, biscuits and cakes is also going well. This is an indicator of clever marketing strategies as well as a trend towards convenience food and westernised dietary patterns.

Among some of the consumers that typically buy organic food, Kirana stores have lost much of their importance due to increasing mobility and changing shopping preferences. The biggest advantage of traditional retail formats such as Kirana stores and street vendors is their proximity to consumer's places of residence or work, and their low-energy infrastructure. They can supply food at cheaper prices and in a more energy-efficient way than modern retail formats. In light of the relatively small contribution that the farming system and transportation make to the overall environmental impact[44], efforts for limiting energy-intensive consumption patterns, promoting traditional crops and expanding climate-friendly retailing formats are of particular relevance. Since their social acceptance is still higher than that for supermarkets, traditional retail formats could also help making organic food available to broader sections of the population, including those that are as yet unaware of organic food or unable to afford the premium prices in supermarkets and organic stores. These systems can also be seen as more socially sustainable because they create more jobs in decentralised retailing.

Several respondents said they would be interested in home delivery of organic food. The concept is already very common in Hyderabad; anything from drinking water to fast food and restaurant meals or supermarket shopping can be delivered, often free of charge or for a minimum purchase amount. 24-Letter-Mantra offers home delivery, and so do some conventional supermarkets. Most consumers interviewed by Lohr and Dittrich (2007) in Kirana stores make use of the delivery service, which is offered by two-thirds of

---

[44] cf. Chapter 2.

the Kirana owners interviewed by them. The most common means of transport used for home delivery are two-wheelers, or for bulky items like drinking water small motorised cargo rickshaws. Home delivery is a strategy well worth looking into for decentralised organic food supply. For example, street vendors could tap the considerable potential for home delivery by engaging in a system where farmers supply directly to them and they deliver products to people's home by pushcart.

Innovative initiatives like the new organic farmer's market in Mumbai provide interesting examples of how organic food can be marketed successfully. It would be worthwhile to explore potential approaches and success factors for similar initiatives in Hyderabad. SERP has several plans for opening more outlets in other locations and for launching new direct marketing channels. In cooperation with MEPMA, a government programme for eliminating urban poverty, they are planning to set up urban kiosks run by farmers that will sell rice, pulses, vegetables and milk. They are also considering opening an outlet at NTR Nagar vegetable market. Currently there are no plans for organic stalls at urban Rythu Bazaars, since there is no permission for setting up new stalls. SERP are also planning to look into home delivery schemes in the future.

In between the two poles of market-oriented organic companies and farmer-centric initiatives there are several mixed forms such as social enterprises and for-profit farmer-owned companies like Chetna Organic. Also, commercial organic companies that have a strong focus on urban consumer markets do not necessarily neglect rural development. The extent to which they really benefit smallholder producers by way of fair producer prices, good labour conditions and strengthening of rural communities has to be carefully evaluated for each individual case. For example, Ecofarms Pvt. Ltd. in Mumbai who supply to Metro Cash and Carry in Hyderabad are a long-established family run business and place strong emphasis on smallholder producer involvement and their livelihood security.

A development towards a highly industrialised organic agriculture sector is not to be expected in India in the near future. Several factors prevent a rapid intensification and industrialisation of the sector: With an average farm size of 3.3 acres (FAS 2009), Indian agriculture is dominated by resource-poor smallholder producers (Partap 2006); 70 % of cultivated area are under rain-fed farming systems (Menon, Sema, and Partap 2010: 77); inadequate rural infrastructure prevents efficient and successful marketing. Nevertheless, the dominant trend in India is towards producing organic food as part of a commercialised commodity chain that has consumer preferences and profit margins in view at least as much as the sustainability of the farming system. Anshu and Mehta (n.y.) recommend two strategies for increasing the profit for farmers: Firstly, economies of scale, and secondly efficiency in the system. At present, the growth prospects of the corporate retail model that relies on economies of scale appear greater. As the scope of the organic market increases, prices will go down in the long run due to more competition and larger volumes of production. According to CSA it is not unlikely that a development similar to the market in Germany will take place, where a big market for cheap, minimal-standard organic products has emerged. In the mid to long term, both models are likely to co-exist. Business-oriented models that combine targeting the export markets with a strong focus on upmarket domestic target groups will prevail in quantitative terms of market share due to greater profit margins in these segments as well as a government policy that supports agribusiness. Direct marketing initiatives and producer-consumer alliances are likely to remain a small but dynamic niche within the organic niche.

The President of ICCOA, Mukesh Gupta, says in a promotional video for the BioFach India trade fair: "BioFach India is significant for the transformation of organic agriculture which was farmer-centric to now business-/ industry-oriented. That's a big achievement."[45] Of course, whether this development is interpreted an achievement of a risk for small-scale farmers depends on the point of view. While it is true that "farming on massive scale will reduce the cost of inputs and labour [...and] also help in reducing the certification cost" (Anshu and Mehta n.y.), part of the sustainability of organic farming lies exactly in its small scale, low level of technology and short nutrient cycles. In a commercial, primarily profit-oriented, industrial-scale mode of organic production it is generally not organic farmers or small organic shops that benefit from the growth of the market, but mainly large food corporations and a few big farmers (Unbekannt 2006). An organic movement that operates according to the principles and strict standards of the original ideas of organic farming rather than for commercial profit and at an industrial scale is the most promising strategy in light of efforts of making the urban food system more sustainable and climate-friendly. A holistic approach to organic farming can make sure that environmental, social and economic benefits are maximised, rather than just exploiting a new marketing niche.

At least part of the consumers buying organic are motivated more by a certain lifestyle and image conveyed by organic shops than by informed support for organic farming. The majority of consumers are not dedicated enough to compromise on price or convenience for the sake of environmental benefits or social concerns for producers. Therefore, the

---

[45] www.biofach-india.com/en/impressions

potential for marketing organic food as more environmentally and climate friendly or more socially responsible in the upmarket, lifestyle-oriented target group seems limited. Motivations of consumers buying from small farmer direct marketing initiatives also include health consciousness, but there is also a potential for raising awareness among consumers of the benefits of traditional and sustainable agricultural practices for the environment, the farmers *and* the consumers. There is a potential for high-priced products if consumers feel the prices are justified by high product quality. While the majority of consumers buying in organic stores belong to the upper middle and upper class, direct marketing with its more moderate price levels could potentially reach broader strata of the population. High price levels prevent many consumers even in the high-income groups from purchasing (more) organic food. If it is to be truly sustainable in a strict sense, sustainable consumption cannot remain a privilege of the well-off. This means that organic products have to be reasonably priced to reach a broader population. Consumers also need to be made aware of the reasons for the higher prices, such as increased labour effort, smaller production scale or fair prices for farmers. One way of achieving this can be closer links between producers and consumers in a localised food system.

## 6.3 Supporting Farmers and Strengthening Regional Food Networks

Improved consumer awareness of organic food will lead to increased demand for organic food. At this stage, the retail infrastructure and organic product supply are still insufficient for meeting even the existing demand. The organic market sector is not growing at the rate that might be expected in light of the significant demand observed by market research (Rao et al. 2006). The owner of Vijaya Enterprises said: "If there was more supply and farmers would manage to bring produce regularly I could easily sell it. I'd also be interested in selling organic vegetables, but it is difficult to get supplies. Everybody wants organic, but it is hard to supply it." Retailers are in fact wary of advertising organic products more actively because they would not be able to satisfy the ensuing demand. Thus one of the sticking points for the future development of the organic market of Hyderabad will be sufficient supply of organic products. The organic retail sector needs greater quantities of production and more consistent supply of high quality in order to keep up its growth rate.

The market for organic food is growing globally, but farmers in developing countries are not well aware of this opportunity (Garibay and Jyoti 2003). At present, government support for organic agriculture in India focuses on large, export-oriented producers. For small farmers, support for sustainable agriculture and marketing initiatives is restricted to a small number of dedicated rural development NGOs. They need better access to information, technical training and financial support to help them during the difficult conversion period. More support for sustainable agriculture, farmer cooperatives and small-farmer marketing initiatives will be vital for developing the domestic market for organic food in a sustainable manner that benefits not only organic food companies and well-off urban consumers but also rural communities and larger segments of the urban population.

It is difficult for small farmers operating individually to supply to supermarkets and organic stores in order to reach more consumers. In order for them to sell directly to supermarkets they have to be able to supply continuously, in large quantities, and consistent quality (cf. CIAS 1999). Cooperatives are one option for farmers that allows them to meet these requirements, however, most farmers do not aspire to sell to supermarkets since the profit margins are small compared to direct marketing. If more supermarkets cooperated directly with farmers cooperatives, farmers could get a higher share of profits, supply chains would become shorter and more energy-efficient, and supermarkets could advertise the environmental benefits and support for the regional economy.

While supermarkets and commercial organic stores will play an important role in bringing more organic products to the consumers, a more comprehensive approach to sustainable food system development is taken by initiatives aiming to strengthen the linkages and networks between producers and urban consumers, for example in the form of Community-Supported Agriculture schemes and producer-consumer partnerships like Sahaja Aharam. The German organic chain LPG is an example of a consumer cooperative that evolved into a larger, economically successful chain that supports small and regional organic marketing initiatives while at the same time reaching large sections of urban consumers. Bhattacharyya (2004: 164f) recommends several strategies for developing the domestic market for organic products, among them development of direct marketing channels such as home-delivery systems, registration of consumers for supplying organic products, and mobile sales near people's work places. Making organic food available in more decentralised localities nearer people's homes or increasing the level of utilisation of home delivery in bulk is more energy efficient, and it will make organic products available to a broader population than at present.

Together with low-input production systems, a decentralised, local food system with short supply chains can minimise fossil fuel consumption through reduced transportation. Alternative retail formats such as direct marketing on farmers' markets, home delivery by low-emission modes of transport, and decentralised marketing by Kirana stores, street vendors, farmer cooperatives and consumer cooperatives have a lower environmental impact. Efficient systems of production and distribution with a reduced number of intermediaries will help making the food system more sustainable as well as increasing profit for farmers. Furthermore, direct interaction between producers and consumers can be an important communication channel for information about organic food for consumers. In India, many consumers are wary of concepts like official certification due to widespread corruption. Therefore personal trust in the producer and retailer is a lot more important for purchasing decisions than official labels. While organic certification will certainly help organic products to increase their market share in the organised retail sector, transparency and participation might be more successfully promoted in the Indian context by building closer links between producers and consumers in local and regional food networks.

## 6.4 Further Research

On the production and marketing side, future research could analyse in more detail the different models of organic food distribution identified in this study. A systematic inventory of delivery systems and a comparison with other cities where market availability and the organic movement in general are more advanced could provide a more detailed picture of the current state of the market in Hyderabad. Further, the sustainability impact of different models of organic food distribution should be substantiated by additional data on production, supply chains and retailing. This would allow a detailed, site-specific ecological footprint analysis for specific food items and for various modes of production, supply chains and retailing. More in-depth research focussing on the production side and on supply chain organisation could provide insights into the impact of different marketing models on smallholder producers' livelihood security and on rural communities in general.

On the consumption side, a detailed survey of the attitudes and purchasing criteria of bulk buyers such as the hospitality industry, large canteens or government institutions could provide deeper insights into the potential for increasing organic sales in this area and for reaching a broader spectrum of the population than through retail. While in Europe sustainable procurement is an important and increasingly popular concept, government policy in India has yet to develop in that field.

A closer analysis of food-related attitudes and values of private sector consumers could add a valuable dimension to the outline of the socio-economic profile and socio-cultural background of consumers developed in this study. In particular, the target group analysis should be substantiated in order to develop strategies for promoting sustainable consumption in an effective, target-group-specific way. Strategies that are well-established in other regions of the world can be taken as an example, but have to be adapted to the specific local context. Such strategies should build upon existing models that link consumers and producers and strengthen participatory regional food networks. The willingness of consumers to engage in producer-consumer networks and direct marketing efforts should be assessed in order to provide an indication of their future potential. To date, there has been very limited experience with such initiatives in Hyderabad. The extent and sustainability of response to the consumer cooperative launched by CSA and the cooperative store opened in 2009 remain to be seen. The long-standing involvement of CSA with both producers and consumers of organic products certainly promises a high degree of sustainability. Further in-depth research would be needed to assess the potential scale to which such initiatives could grow in Hyderabad.

To date, the demand for organic food is growing mainly in a small section of the population. Accordingly, this study focused mainly on middle and high-income, highly educated consumers who were already aware of organic foods. Attitudes towards organic products and the financial margins for purchasing them among lower-income groups are important for future market growth and also for efforts for making organic food more socially inclusive, so that organic does not become part of an elitist luxury lifestyle but a mass movement for sustainability.

# References

Adhavani, R. (2009). Women vow to fight against GM crops: Mobile bio-diversity festival concludes. *The Hindu*, February 14.

Anshu, Kumari and Mehta, Jitender (no year). Promotion of organic food. Opportunities & Challenges: National Institute of Agricultural Marketing. www.indiabschools.com/Promotion%20of%20Organic%20Foods.pdf [15-01-09].

Asan, Yildiz (2008). Klimafreundlich einkaufen. www.nachhaltigkeit.org/20081114491/materialien-produkte/hintergrund/klimafreundlich-einkaufen [05-03-09].

Barrett, John; Birch, Rachel; Cherrett, Nia and Wiedmann, Thomas (2005). Exploring the application of the ecological footprint to sustainable consumption policy. *Journal of Environmental Policy and Planning* 7(4): 303–316.

Benoît, Catherine and Mazijn, Bernard (eds.) (2009). *Guidelines for Social Life Cycle Assessment of Products*. UNEP. www.unep.fr/scp/publications/details.asp?id=DTI/1164/PA [01-10-09].

Bhattacharyya, P (2004). *Organic Food Production in India: Status, Strategy and Scope*. Jodhpur: Agrobios.

Bilharz, Michael (2007). Key Points nachhaltigen Konsums. In: Belz, Frank-Martin; Karg, Georg and Witt, Dieter (eds.). *Nachhaltiger Konsum und Verbraucherpolitik im 21. Jahrhundert*. Wirtschaftswissenschaftliche Nachhaltigkeitsforschung, Vol. 1. Marburg: Metropolis-Verlag, 105–138.

Bilharz, Michael (2009). *"Key Points" nachhaltigen Konsums: Ein strukturpolitisch fundierter Strategieansatz für die Nachhaltigkeitskommunikation im Kontext aktivierender Verbraucherpolitik*. Wirtschaftswissenschaftliche Nachhaltigkeitsforschung, Vol. 4. Marburg: Metropolis-Verlag.

Bogun, Roland (2008). Nachhaltigkeitsdiskurs, Umwelt- und Risikobewusstsein: Ansatzpunkte für ein nachhaltig(er)es Konsumentenverhalten? In: Lange, Hellmuth (ed.). *Nachhaltigkeit als radikaler Wandel: Die Quadratur des Kreises?* Wiesbaden: VS Verlag für Sozialwissenschaften, 123–147.

Bourdieu, Pierre (2002) [1984]. *Distinction: A Social Critique of the Judgement of Taste*. Reprint. London: Routledge.

Brand, Karl Werner (2008). Konsum im Kontext. Der "verantwortliche Konsument" - ein Motor nachhaltigen Konsums? In: Lange, Hellmuth (ed.). *Nachhaltigkeit als radikaler Wandel: Die Quadratur des Kreises?* Wiesbaden: VS Verlag für Sozialwissenschaften, 71–93.

Brunner, Karl-Michael (2009). Nachhaltiger Konsum: Am Beispiel des Essens. *Sozialwissenschaftliche Studiengesellschaft: SWS-Rundschau* 49: 29–49.

Cannon, Terry (2002). Food Security, Food Systems and Livelihoods: Competing Explanations of Hunger. *Die Erde* 133(4): 345–362.

Carroll, Arati Menon (2005). India's Booming Organic Food Bazaar. www.ia.rediff.com /money/2005/oct/17spec1.htm [15-01-09].

Chakrabarti, Somnath and Baisya, Rajat K (2007). Purchase Motivations and Attitudes of Organic Food Buyers. *Decision* 34(1): 2–22.

Chander, M. (1997). Organic Farming: Towards Sustainable Agricultural Development. *Social Action* 47(1): 216–230.

CIAS (1995). Regional Food Systems Research: Needs, Priorities, and Recommendations. Centre for Integrated Agricultural Systems. www.cias.wisc.edu/farm-to-fork/regional-food-systems-research-needs-priorities-and-recommendations/ [03-05-09].

CIAS (1999). *New Markets for Producers: Selling to Retail Stores.* Research Brief, Vol. 38. Centre for Integrated Agricultural Systems. www.cias.wisc.edu/farm-to-fork/new-markets-for-producers-selling-to-retail-stores [04-05-09].

Cole, C.V.; Duxbury, J.; Freney, J.; Heinemeyer, O.; Minami, K.; Mosier, A.; Paustian, K. et al. (1997). Global Estimates of Potential Mitigation of Greenhouse Gas Emissions by Agriculture. *Nutrient Cycling in Agroecosystems* 49: 221–228.

Collins, Andrea and Fairchild, Ruth (2007). Sustainable Food Consumption at a Sub-National Level: An Ecological Footprint, Nutritional and Economic Analysis. *Journal of Environmental Policy and Planning* 9(1): 5–26.

Collins, Andrea; Flynn, Andrew and Netherwood, Alan (2005). *Reducing Cardiff's Ecological Footprint.* Cardiff. www.brass.cf.ac.uk/projects/Measuring_Reporting _and_Learning/progress-towards-sustainability–Ecological-Footprinting–Cardiff-Footprint .html [25-05-10].

DDS (2008). *Farmer-Proofing Agricultural Research: Current Trends in India. A Fact Sheet.* Democratising Agriculture Series, Vol. 1. Hyderabad: Deccan Development Society.

DeWeerdt, Sarah (2009). Is Local Food Better? Worldwatch Institute. www.worldwatch .org/node/6064?emc=el&m=227941&l=4&v=0c378b5401 [30-04-09].

Dharmadhikary, Shripad (2010). Chemical-Free Food: Organic Veggies in my Inbox. www.indiatogether.org [18-06-10].

Enneking, Ulrich; Franz, Rainer and Profeta, Adriano (2007). Nachhaltigkeitssegmente in den Bedarfsfeldern Ernährung, Wohnen und Mobilität. In: Belz, Frank-Martin; Karg, Georg and Witt, Dieter (Eds.). *Nachhaltiger Konsum und Verbraucherpolitik im 21. Jahrhundert*. Wirtschaftswissenschaftliche Nachhaltigkeitsforschung, Vol. 1. Marburg: Metropolis-Verlag, 79–103.

Eyhorn, Frank (2005). Success Story: Organic India. In: Willer, Helga and Yussefi, Minou (Eds.). *The World of Organic Agriculture: Statistics and Emerging Trends 2005*. Bonn and Frick (CH): International Federation of Organic Agriculture Movements (IFOAM) and Research Institute of Organic Agriculture (FiBL), 74–75.

FAS (2009). India: Agricultural Economy and Policy Report. USDA Foreign Agricultural Service (FAS), January. www.fas.usda.gov/country/India/Indian%20Agricultural%20Economy%20and%20Policy%20Paper.pdf [18-05-10].

Foodwatch (2008). Organic: A Climate Saviour? The foodwatch report on the greenhouse effect of conventional and organic farming in Germany. Based on the study "The Impact of German Agriculture on the Climate" by the Institute for Ecological Economy Research (IÖW). www.foodwatch.de/foodwatch/content/e6380/e24459/e24474/foodwatch_report_on_the_greenhouse_effect_of_farming_08_2008_ger.pdf [18-04-09].

Franz, Rainer (2006). *Nachhaltigkeitsmilieus in den Bedürfnisfeldern Ernährung, Wohnen, Mobilität*. Consumer Science Diskussionsbeitrag Nr. 6. Weihenstephan: Technische Universität München. www.mcr.wi.tum.de/142.html [12-10-09].

Garibay, Salvador V. and Jyoti, Katke (2003). Market Opportunities and Challenges for Indian Organic Products. http://orgprints.org/00002684 [15-01-09].

Geden, Oliver (2009). Strategischer Konsum statt nachhaltiger Politik? Ohnmacht und Selbstüberschätzung des "klimabewussten" Verbrauchers. *Transit - Europäische Revue* 36 (Winter 2008/2009), 132-141. www.swp-berlin.org/brennpunkte/dossier.php?id=9606&PHPSESSID=f0f74 [22-04-09].

Ghosh, Padmaparna (2007). Nine states want to cash in on organic crops: Organic farming is working out in states which have a higher percentage of smaller farmers. *livemint.com*, September 6. www.livemint.com/2007/09/06000706/9-states-want-to-cash-in-on-or.html [15-03-10].

Götz, Konrad (2001). Sozial-ökologische Typologisierung zwischen Zielgruppensegmentation und Sozialstrukturanalyse. In: Haan, Gerhard de; Lantermann, Ernst-Dieter; Linneweber, Volker and Reusswig, Fritz (eds.). *Typenbildung in der sozialwissenschaftlichen Umweltforschung*. Lehrtexte Soziologie. Opladen: Leske & Budrich, 127–138.

Government of India (2000). National Agricultural Policy. Department of Agriculture and Cooperation, Ministry of Agriculture. www.nls.ac.in/CEERA/ceerafeb04/html/documents/agri.htm [05-08-09].

Government of India (2005). *National Programme for Organic Production.* 6th ed. New Delhi: Department of Commerce, Ministry of Commerce and Industry. www.apeda.com/organic/ORGANIC_CONTENTS/English_Organic_Sept05.pdf [10-03-09].

Griffith, P.L. and Bentley, M.E. (2001). The nutrition transition is underway: India. *Journal for Nutrition* 131(10): 2692–2700.

Hanspal, Savita (2010). Consumer Survey on Sustainable Tea & Coffee Consumption. New Delhi: Partners in Change.

Harish, Ranjani (2003). Indian Dietary Habits: The Changing Trend. *Food & Nutrition World* November, 49–50.

Hayn, Doris (2005). Ernährungsstile: Über die Vielfalt des Ernährungshandelns im Alltag. In: Agrarbündnis e.V. (ed.). *Der Kritische Agrarbericht 2005.* Kassel, Hamm (Westfalen): ABL Bauernblatt Verlags-GmbH, 284-288. www.kritischer-agrarbericht.de [17-11-09].

Hema, Vijay (2010). Go veg to save the globe? *The Hindu*, February 1, Metro Plus.

Hofmann, Rebecca and Dittrich, Christoph (2009). Changing Food Culture in Globalising Hyderabad. Research Reports for Analysis and Action for Sustainable Development of Hyderabad. Berlin: Humboldt-University. www.sustainable-hyderabad.in.

Hofmann, Rebecca and Dittrich, Christoph (2010). The Awareness of Risks in the Field of Food and Nutrition: Perception, valuation and mitigation in the everyday life of Hyderabad's lower middle class women. Research Reports for Analysis and Action for Sustainable Development of Hyderabad. Berlin: Humboldt-University. www.sustainable-hyderbad.in.

Holdinghausen, Heike (2009). Bio erfolgreich im Supermarkt. *die tageszeitung*, February 21.

IBEF (2004). Tapping India's eco-farming potential. Indian Brand Equity Foundation. www.ibef.org/artdisplay.aspx?cat_id=86&art_id=4488 [30-01-09].

Jackson, Tim (Ed.) (2006). *The Earthscan Reader on Sustainable Consumption.* London and Sterling, VA: Earthscan.

Jain, S.K and Kaur, G. (2004). Green Marketing: An Attitudinal and Behavioral Analysis of Indian Consumers. *Global Business Review* 5(2): 187–205.

Kalanidhi, M.L. (2006). The Fast Food Boom (Cover Story). *Wow! Hyderabad* (August), 26–32.

Kalita, Anurag; Doshi, Kopal; Dalmia, Shristi; Baweja, Amit and Shetty, Ashit (2008). Fabindia. Study submitted to Dr. Raja Saxsena, School of Business Management NMIMS. www.scribd.com/doc/11569951/A-Marketing-Project-on-FabIndia [08-05-09].

Kotschi, Johannes and Müller-Sämann, Karl (2004). *The Role of Organic Agriculture in Mitigating Climate Change: A Scoping Study.* Bonn: IFOAM - International Federation of Organic Agriculture Movements.

Lohr, Kerstin and Dittrich, Christoph (2007). Changing Food Purchasing and Consumption Habits among Urban Middle-Classes in Hyderabad. Research Reports for Analysis and Action for Sustainable Development of Hyderabad No. 3. Berlin: Humboldt-University. www.sustainable-hyderabad.in [01-02-09].

Mawdsley, Emma (2004). India's Middle Classes and the Environment. *Development and Change* 25 (1), 79–103.

Menon, Manoj Kumar; Jagannath, S.; Roy, Jaydip and Khare, Sukanya (eds.) (2009). *International Seminar: "India Organic – Strategies to Surge Ahead".* Bangalore: International Competence Centre for Organic Agriculture.

Menon, Manoj Kumar; Sema, Akali and Partap, Tej (2010). India Organic Pathway: Strategies and Experiences. In: Partap, Tej and Saeed, M. (eds.). *Organic Agriculture and Agribusiness: Innovation and Fundamentals.* Tokyo: Asian Productivity Organisation, 75–86. www.apo-tokyo.org/00e-books/AG-22_Organic Agriculture/AG-22_OrganicAgriculture.pdf [31-05-10].

Misra, Savvy Soumya (2009). Made it. Cover Story: Agriculture. *Down to Earth* 16 (January 1-15), 31–38. www.downtoearth.org.in/cover.asp?foldername=20090115 &filename=news&sid=10&sec_id=9 [18-04-09].

Mujeeb-Ur-Rahman and Visweswara Rao, K. (2001). Effect of Socio-Economic Status on Food Consumption Pattern and Nutrient Intake of Adults: A Case Study in Hyderabad. *The Indian Journal for Nutrition and Dietetics* 38(4): 292–300.

NCAER (2005). The Great Indian Market. Results from the NCAER's Market Information Survey on Households. National Council of Applied Economic Research. www.ncaer.org/downloads/PPT/TheGreatIndianMarket.pdf [06-05-09].

Niggli, Urs (2010). High sequestration, low emission, food secure farming - the potential of organic agriculture for climate change mitigation. Presentation at the IFOAM EU Group Organic Day in DG Environment, 20 April 2010.

Niggli, Urs and Fließbach, Andreas (2009). Gut fürs Klima? Ökologische und konventionelle Landwirtschaft im Vergleich. In: Agrarbündnis e.V. (Ed.). *Landwirtschaft 2009: Der kritische Agrarbericht. Schwerpunkt: Landwirtschaft im Klimawandel.* Kassel, Hamm (Westfalen): ABL Bauernblatt Verlags-GmbH, 103-109. www.kritischer-agrarbericht.de [17-11-09].

Niggli, Urs; Fließbach, Andreas; Hepperly, P. and Scialabba, N. (2009). *Low Greenhouse Gas Agriculture: Mitigation and Adaptation Potential of Sustainable Farming Systems.* 2nd ed. Rome: Food and Agricultural Organisation (FAO). ftp://ftp.fao.org/docrep/fao/010/ai781e/ai781e00.pdf [12-05-10].

Niggli, Urs; Leifert, Carlo; Alföldi, Thomas; Lück, Lorna and Willer, Helga (2007). *Improving Sustainability in Organic and Low Input Food Production Systems. Proceedings of the 3rd International Congress of the European Integrated Project Quality Low Input Food (QLIF). University of Hohenheim, Germany, March 20 – 23, 2007.* Hohenheim: University of Hohenheim. http://orgprints.org/10417/ [13-10-09].

Organicfacts (2006). Organic Food Consumption in India. www.organicfacts.net/organic-food/organic-food-trends/organic-food-consumption-in-india.html [16-01-09].

Osswald, Nina and Dittrich, Christoph (2009). The Market for Organic Food in Hyderabad, India: Consumer Attitudes and Marketing Opportunities. Research Reports for Analysis and Action for Sustainable Development of Hyderabad. Berlin: Humboldt-University. www.sustainable-hyderabad.in.

Pai, J.S. (2007). Health Foods: Future of Indian Food Industry. *Indian Food Industry* Nov-Dec, 29–32.

Paradkar, Manish; Sharma, Kirti; Singh, Jasvir and Mallya, R.R. (2007). Ready-to-Eat Foods: Technological Process and Indian Perspective. *Indian Food Industry* Nov-Dec, 39.

Partap, Tej (2006). *The India Organic Pathway: Making Way for Itself.* Occasional Paper, Vol. 1. Bangalore: International Competence Centre for Organic Agriculture.

Polasa, Kalpagam; Sudershan, R.V.; Subba Rao, G.M.; Vishnu Vardhana Rao, M.; Rao, Pratima and Sivakumar, B. (2006). KABP Study on Food and Drug Safety in India: A Report. Hyderabad: Food & Drug Toxicology Research Centre, National Institute of Nutrition.

Pollan, Michael (2006). *The Omnivore's Dilemma: A Natural History of Four Meals.* London/ New York: Penguin.

Prabu, M.J. (2009). A farmer develops an herbal pest repellent after suffering from chemical pesticides: The farmer suffered a severe paralytic stroke for nearly three years. *The Hindu*, February 26.

Prasad, Y.G. (2008). Bio-Intensive Integrated Pest Management in Organic Farming. In: Venkateswarlu, B.; Balloli, S.S. and Ramakrishna, Y.S. (eds.). *Organic Farming in Rainfed Agriculture: Opportunities and Constraints*. Hyderabad: Central Research Institute for Dryland Agriculture, 96–101.

Pretty, J.N. (1995). *Regenerating Agriculture: Policies and Practice for Sustainability and Self-Reliance*. London: Earthscan.

Pütz, Robert and Schröder, Frank (2006). Konsum und Konsumenten in der Geographie. In: Gebhardt, Hans; Glaser, Rüdiger; Radtke, Ulrich and Reuber, Paul (Eds.). *Geographie: Physische Geographie und Humangeographie*. Heidelberg: Spektrum Akademischer Verlag, 911–929.

Raghunatha Rao, D.; Vijayapushpam, T.; Grace Maria Antony, T.; Subba Rao, G.M. and Rameshwar Sarma, K.V. (2004). Nutrition Knowledge on Dietary Habits of School Going Adolescent Girls in Hyderabad. Report of the National Conference on Human Health and Nutrition, Hyderabad, 12.-13.12.2004. Hyderabad.

Rajiv, M. (2009). Busting health-boosting claims. *The Hindu*, April 11, Metro Weekend.

Ramanjaneyulu, D. and Chennamaneni, Ramesh (2007). Pesticides, Residues and Regulation: A Case Study of Vegetables in Hyderabad Market. Research Reports for Analysis and Action for Sustainable Development of Hyderabad No. 10. Berlin: Humboldt-University. www.sustainable-hyderabad.in [15-05-10].

Rao, C.H. Srinivas; Venkateswarlu, V.; Surender, T.; Eddleston, Michael and Buckley, Nick A. (2005). Pesticide Poisoning in South India: Opportunities for Prevention and Improved Medical Management. *Tropical Medicine and International Health* 10(6): 581–588.

Rao, Kishore; Supe, Raj; Menon, Manoj Kumar and Partap, Tej (2006). *The Market for Organic Foods in India: Consumer Perceptions and Market Potential. Findings of a Nation Wide Survey*. Bangalore: International Competence Centre for Organic Agriculture.

Reachout Hyderabad (2008). SPAR launches its 1st Supermarket in Hyderabad. www.reachouthyderabad.com/business/bizretail/spar.htm [18-03-09].

Reusswig, Fritz; Lotze-Campen, Hermann and Gerlinger, Katrin (2005). Changing Global Lifestyle and Consumption Patterns: The Case of Energy and Food. In: Radhakrishna, G. (Ed.). *Consumer Behaviour: Effective measurement tools*. Hyderabad: ICFAI University Press, 197–210.

Richter, Toralf and Kovacs, Annamaria (2005). Strategies to support domestic organic markets in countries with emerging organic sectors. Paper presented at the conference Researching Sustainable Systems - International Scientific Conference on Organic Agriculture, Adelaide, Australia, September 21-23, 2005. http://orgprints.org/4455/ [08-05-09].

Singh, Jagdish (2004). Organic Farming and Agribusiness for Food Security in India. In: Singh, Tapeshwar (Ed.). *Resource Conservation and Food Security: An Indian Experience Vol. I.* Concept Publishing, 277–288.

Singh, Komal Vijay (2009). Nutrition in a packet: The mallscape encompasses a rich array of health foods with consumers making a grab for them. *The Hindu*, February 25, Metro Plus Hyderabad.

Singh, Tapeshwar (Ed.) (2004). *Resource Conservation and Food Security: An Indian Experience Vol. I.* Concept Publishing.

Srivastava, Roli (2009). Supermarkets shut shop, face rent crisis. *The Times of India*, February 5.

Stieß, Immanuel and Hayn, Doris (2005). *Ernährungsstile im Alltag.* Ernährungswende-Diskussionspaper, Vol. 5. Frankfurt am Main: ISOE.

Sudershan, R.V.; Subba Rao, G.M.; Rao, Pratima; Vardhana, M. Vishnu and Polasa, Kalpagam (2008). Food safety related perceptions and practices of mothers: A case study in Hyderabad, India. *Food Control* 19(5): 506–513.

Tewari, G.M. (2007). New Concepts and Innovations in Food & Beverage Industry. *Indian Food Industry* Nov-Dec, 33–37.

Thaler, Richard H. and Sunstein, Cass R. (2009). *Nudge: Improving Decisions About Health, Wealth, and Happiness.* Revised. Penguin, February 24.

The Hindu (2009). Organic vegetables up for grabs. *The Hindu*, January 28.

The Nielsen Company (2006). Indians Amongst the Top 10 Buyers of Foods with 'Health Supplements' Globally but Lack Access to Organic Food Products. http://in.nielsen.com/news/20060220.shtml [16-01-09].

The Nielsen Company (2007). Unavailability and price the major reasons for Indians not purchasing organic products. http://in.nielsen.com/news/20071203.shtml [16-01-09].

UN (2000). United Nations Millennium Declaration. Resolution adopted by the General Assembly. www.un.org/millennium/declaration/ares552e.htm [18-06-10].

Unbekannt, Irina (2006). Brauchen wir eine neue Bio-Bewegung? Regionale Kreislaeufe fuer Lebensqualitaet statt globaler Kreislaeufe fuer Profit. *Allercon-News* 6. www.bio100.de/html/body_11_archiv.html [05-05-09].

UNEP/ UNCTAD (2008). Organic Agriculture and Food Security in Africa. United Nations. New York and Geneva: UNEP-UNCTAD Capacity-building Task Force on Trade, Environment and Development. www.unctad.org/en/docs/ditcted200715 _en.pdf [01-05-10].

Venetoulis, Jason and Talberth, John (2008). Refining the Ecological Footprint. *Environment, Development and Sustainability* 10(4): 441–469.

Vijayapushpam, T.; Menon, K.K.; Raghunatha Rao, D. and Maria Antony, G. (2003). A qualitative assessment of nutrition knowledge levels and dietary intake of schoolchildren in Hyderabad. *Public Health Nutrition* 6: 683- 8.

von Koerber, K.; Kretschmer, J.; Prinz, S. and Dasch, E. (2009). Globale Nahrungssicherung für eine wachsende Weltbevölkerung: Flächenbedarf und Klimarelevanz sich wandelnder Ernährungsgewohnheiten. *Journal für Verbraucherschutz und Lebensmittelsicherheit* 4(2): 174–189.

von Koerber, Karl and Kretschmer, Juergen (2009). Ernährung und Klima: Nachhaltiger Konsum ist ein Beitrag zum Klimaschutz. In: Agrarbündnis e.V. (ed.). *Landwirtschaft 2009: Der kritische Agrarbericht. Schwerpunkt: Landwirtschaft im Klimawandel.* Kassel, Hamm (Westfalen): ABL Bauernblatt Verlags-GmbH, 280–285. www.kritischer-agrarbericht.de [17-11-09].

Wackernagel, Mathis and Rees, William E. (1996). *Our Ecological Footprint: Reducing Human Impact on the Earth.* Gabriola Island: New Society Publishers.

Wikipedia (2009). Local Food. http://en.wikipedia.org/wiki/Local_food [08-05-09].

WWF (2008). *Living Planet Report 2008.* Gland, Switzerland: World Wildlife Fund for Nature. www.panda.org/livingplanet [25-05-10].